The World Bank

From reconstruction to development
to equity

Katherine Marshall

Routledge
Taylor & Francis Group

LONDON AND NEW YORK

First published 2008
by Routledge
2 Park Square, Milton Park, Abingdon, Oxon OX14 4RN

Simultaneously published in the USA and Canada
by Routledge
270 Madison Avenue, New York, NY 10016

Routledge is an imprint of the Taylor & Francis Group, an informa business

© 2008 Katherine Marshall

Reprinted 2008, 2009

Typeset in Times New Roman by
Taylor & Francis Books
Printed and bound in Great Britain by
the MPG Books Group

British Library Cataloguing in Publication Data
A catalogue record for this book is available from the British Library

Library of Congress Cataloging in Publication Data
A catalog record for this book has been requested

ISBN 978-0-415-38128-4 (hbk)
ISBN 978-0-415-38132-1 (pbk)
ISBN 978-0-203-96753-9 (ebk)

The World Bank

Created in 1944, at the same time as the International Monetary Fund (IMF) but before the founding of the United Nations (UN), the World Bank is a global cooperative of 185 (as of 2007) member countries.

The original and core institution—what is often called the "World Bank"—is the International Bank for Reconstruction and Development (IBRD), which makes loans to countries that are creditworthy. In 1956 the International Finance Corporation (IFC) joined the IBRD to work directly with the private sector. And in 1960 the International Development Association (IDA) was established with the mandate of serving the world's poorest countries and communities. Other affiliates provide investment guarantees and work to resolve investment disputes. Together the five distinct institutions are known as the World Bank group. Today, the World Bank aspires to be the world's premier development institution. Its credo is captured by the bold phrase at the front entrance to its headquarters: "Our dream is a world free of poverty." Its mandate is to work with the world's poorer countries—some 100 today—to further their economic and social development. It does this by providing a combination of financial resources, technical support, advice and analysis, training, and coordination of development assistance. In practice the World Bank is deeply involved in virtually every facet of development, and is a major actor both in countries that seek its support and partnership and in the development community at large.

This book provides a practical introduction to the multifaceted work of the World Bank. It sets this work—as well as the controversies it has provoked—in a historical context, and lays out an agenda for the years ahead.

Katherine Marshall is Senior Fellow at Georgetown University's Berkley Center for Religion, Peace and World Affairs and Visiting Professor in the Government Department. She worked for 35 years at the World Bank in a wide range of positions and regions.

Routledge Global Institutions

Edited by Thomas G. Weiss
The CUNY Graduate Center, New York, USA
and Rorden Wilkinson
University of Manchester, UK

About the Series

The Global Institutions Series is designed to provide readers with comprehensive, accessible, and informative guides to the history, structure, and activities of key international organizations. Every volume stands on its own as a thorough and insightful treatment of a particular topic, but the series as a whole contributes to a coherent and complementary portrait of the phenomenon of global institutions at the dawn of the millennium.

Books are written by recognized experts, conform to a similar structure, and cover a range of themes and debates common to the series. These areas of shared concern include the general purpose and rationale for organizations, developments over time, membership, structure, decision-making procedures, and key functions. Moreover, current debates are placed in historical perspective alongside informed analysis and critique. Each book also contains an annotated bibliography and guide to electronic information as well as any annexes appropriate to the subject matter at hand.

The volumes currently published or under contract include:

The United Nations and Human Rights (2005)
A guide for a new era
by Julie Mertus (American University)

The UN Secretary General and Secretariat (2005)
by Leon Gordenker (Princeton University)

United Nations Global Conferences (2005)
by Michael G. Schechter (Michigan State University)

The UN General Assembly (2005)
by M.J. Peterson (University of Massachusetts, Amherst)

Internal Displacement (2006)
Conceptualization and its consequences
by Thomas G. Weiss (The CUNY Graduate Center) and David A. Korn

Global Environmental Institutions (2006)
by Elizabeth R. DeSombre (Wellesley College)

The Regional Development Banks
Lending with a regional flavor
by Jonathan R. Strand (University of Nevada, Las Vegas)

Multilateral Cooperation Against Terrorism
by Peter Romaniuk (John Jay College of Criminal Justice, CUNY)

Transnational Organized Crime
by Frank Madsen (University of Cambridge)

Pacebuilding
From concept to commission
by Robert Jenkins (University of London)

For further information regarding the series, please contact:

Craig Fowlie, Publisher, Politics & International Studies
Taylor & Francis
2 Park Square, Milton Park, Abingdon
Oxford OX14 4RN, UK

+44 (0)207 842 2057 Tel
+44 (0)207 842 2302 Fax

Craig.Fowlie@tandf.co.uk
www.routledge.com

For Laura and Patrick,
who have lived the World Bank from the start

Contents

Illustrations

Boxes

Foreword

The current volume is the twenty-first in a dynamic series on "global institutions." The series strives (and, based on the volumes published to date, succeeds) to provide readers with definitive guides to the most visible aspects of what we know as "global governance." Remarkable as it may seem, there exist relatively few books that offer in-depth treatments of prominent global bodies, processes and associated issues, much less an entire series of concise and complementary volumes. Those that do exist are either out of date, inaccessible to the non-specialist reader, or seek to develop a specialized understanding of particular aspects of an institution or process rather than offer an overall account of its functioning. Similarly, existing books have often been written in highly technical language or have been crafted "in-house" and are notoriously self-serving and narrow.

The advent of electronic media has undoubtedly helped research and teaching by making data and primary documents of international organizations more widely available, but it has also complicated matters. The growing reliance on the Internet and other electronic methods of finding information about key international organizations and processes has served, ironically, to limit the quality of educational and analytical materials to which most readers have ready access—namely, books. Public relations documents, raw data, and loosely refereed web sites do not make for intelligent analysis. Official publications compete with a vast amount of electronically available information, much of which is suspect because of its ideological or self-promoting slant. Paradoxically, a growing range of purportedly independent web sites offering analyses of the activities of particular organizations has emerged, but one inadvertent consequence has been to frustrate access to basic, authoritative, readable, critical, and well-researched texts. The market for such has actually been reduced by the ready availability of varying quality electronic materials.

For those of us who teach, research, and practice in the area, such access to information has been particularly frustrating. We thus were delighted when Routledge saw the value of a series that bucks this trend and provides key reference points to the most significant global institutions and issues. They know that serious students and professionals want serious analyses. We have assembled a first-rate line-up of authors to address that market. Our intention is to provide one-stop shopping for all readers—students (both undergraduate and postgraduate), negotiators, diplomats, practitioners from nongovernmental and intergovernmental organizations, and interested parties alike—seeking information about most prominent institutional aspects of global governance.

The World Bank

The World Bank has a reputation that few organizations can boast and fewer still would court. Lambasted by the left as an instrument of corporate capital and decried by the right for being soft on corruption and government intervention, yet nonetheless celebrated by its supporters as a brave and innovative development institution, "the Bank" divides opinion like no other. It has become notorious for recent political scandals—for example, the departures of chief economist Joseph Stiglitz, who subsequently won the Nobel Prize in Economic Sciences, in 2000 and of president Paul Wolfowitz in 2007 as these pages were being finalized. The headlines surrounding these events along with its weighted system of voting and bankrolling of controversial projects are probably as familiar to readers as its approach to development.

The magnitude of its resources—disbursing some $25 billion annually—dwarfs other United Nations (UN) institutions. The Bank can claim a near monopoly on the *business* of development (in a way that the United Nations Development Programme cannot);[1] moreover, it is a partner institution, and leading player in institutional responses to climate change (through the Global Environment Facility) and fighting the spread of infectious disease (through the Multi-Country AIDS Program). It is not just *the* development institution; it is a core agency of global governance.

It was not always this way. The Bank began life as one-third of an economic triumvirate—reflecting John Maynard Keynes's vision of the International Bank for Reconstruction and Development (IBRD), the International Monetary Fund (IMF), and the still-born International Trade Organization that subsequently saw life as the General Agreement on Tariffs and Trade (GATT) and finally the World Trade

Organization (WTO) in 1995. Based on his exposure to and analysis of the failure to move beyond the revenge in the Treaty of Versailles following World War I, the twentieth-century's most famous economist designed the three institutions to bring certainty to a war-damaged and depression-ravaged world economy.[2] Like the IMF, the Bank's original remit was to assist in the reconstruction of Europe—echoed in its original name, the IBRD (which forms the core of the current World Bank group). However, the rapid onset of the Cold War saw the work of both the Bank and the Fund circumscribed by the Marshall Plan—a huge package of assistance lent by the United States (with a little Canadian assistance) to Western Europe to assist in industrial reconstruction and the reinforcement of the Western alliance as a viable alternative to the Soviet Union and the Warsaw Pact.

Marshall aid proved only to be a temporary setback for the Bank as the dramatic and rapid decolonization of the post-war period provided the institution with an opportunity to become *the* lender to the developing world. The change of focus away from Europe and reconstruction toward what is now called the Global South's industrialization and development illustrated for the first time a tendency in the Bank toward institutional adaptation and innovation—followed thereafter by such intellectual switches from brick-and-mortar construction to investments in people and the creation of such institutions as the International Finance Corporation (IFC) in 1956 to support the private sector and the International Development Association (IDA) in 1960 to provide credits instead of loans to poor countries. While many critics argue that the Bank's system of governance has remained anachronistic (based on financial might rather than the one-country one-vote system prevalent throughout the UN system), it has nevertheless continually sought to reflect and build upon the pursuit of an ever-more comprehensive approach to development (albeit this has also been the source of much criticism). More often than not, this dynamism has been associated with its executive head—a feature of the Bank about which Robert Zoellick, who became the institution's eleventh president in June 2007, will be only too aware.

For all of its dynamism, power, and controversy, the Bank remains little understood. Although its policies are well known and frequently scrutinized, its internal workings are seldom explored. Although there are in-depth histories,[3] as strange as it may seem, almost no nuts-and-bolts accounts of the Bank exist.

We were delighted then when Katherine Marshall agreed to write this book for us, completing our coverage of Keynes's economic triumvirate.[4] Katherine is currently Senior Fellow and Visiting Professor at Georgetown University's Berkley Center for Religion, Peace and World Affairs, and also serves as senior advisor for the World Bank. She is a veteran of more than three decades in the field of international development most in the employ of the World Bank. Few know the institution as well as she does. As outsiders who look at the Bank from afar, we tend to see mainly the warts on the institutional apparatus and listen closely to critics who question whether the last six decades of development efforts have been counterproductive.[5] As an insider until recently, Katherine brings to bear a very passionate and informed perspective that is far from that of a cheerleader. She is balanced and fair in her approach and has crafted an expert guide to the Bank that draws upon her extensive experience—complete with a host of engaging stories and anecdotes to illustrate her more general points. Given the Bank's place in contemporary global governance, and the expertise with which it is written, this book is required reading for all. As always, we welcome comments from our readers.

Thomas G. Weiss, The CUNY Graduate Center, New York, USA
Rorden Wilkinson, University of Manchester, UK
December 2007

Acknowledgments

This book owes large debts to colleagues and critics, especially World Bank friends and colleagues over 35 years, far too many to name. My frequent presentations both to new World Bank staff and other widely varied audiences, aimed to explain the mysteries of the World Bank, in many respects provided the germ of this book. These participants, as well as my students at Georgetown and George Washington Universities and the University of Cambodia, sharpened my thinking about how the Bank was supposed to work juxtaposed with how it was perceived. Laura Blinkhorn, Tom Blinkhorn, John Clark, Paul Cadario, Scott Guggenheim, Jeff Guttman, Werner Kiene, David Lindauer, Stephen McGroarty, Craig Murphy, and (especially) Heike Reichelt and Marisa Van Saanen gave practical and thoughtful suggestions on the draft manuscript. Nicholas Krafft provided stalwart support for the project and Jan-Marie Hopkins helped with many administrative hurdles. Sandra Hackman went through the manuscript with a tough editor's mind. I am grateful particularly to Rorden Wilkinson and Thomas Weiss, the creative and diligent series editors, for supporting my involvement in the project and for their incisive observations. My beloved children have offered the bluntest imaginable views of the World Bank's pretensions, though its poverty mission gripped their imaginations from the beginning. Their questions over 27 years about mission, organization, and things practical taught me much of what I know.

Abbreviations

AAA	Analytic and Advisory Activities
ADB	Asian Development Bank
AfDB	African Development Bank
AiDA	Accessible Information on Development Activities
APEC	Asia-Pacific Economic Cooperation
ASEM	Asia Europe Meeting
CABEI	Central American Bank for Economic Integration
CAF	Corporación Andina de Fomento
CARE	Cooperative for Relief and Assistance Everywhere
CAS	Country Assistance Strategy
CDB	Caribbean Development Bank
CDF	Comprehensive Development Framework
CFA	Communauté Financière Africaine (African Financial Community)
CGAP	Consultative Group to Assist the Poor
COMIBOL	Corporación Minera de Bolivia
CPIA	Country Policy And Institutional Assessment
DGF	Development Gateway Foundation
DGF	Development Grants Facility
EADB	East African Development Bank
EBRD	European Bank for Reconstruction and Development
ECOSOC	Economic and Social Council (of the United Nations)
EIB	European Investment Bank
ESF	Emergency Social Fund
FAO	United Nations Food and Agriculture Organization
GDG	Global Development Gateway
GDN	Global Development Network
GEF	Global Environment Facility
HIPC	Highly Indebted Poor Country Initiative

HIV/AIDS	human immunodeficiency virus/acquired immunodeficiency syndrome
IADB	Interamerican Development Bank
IBRD	International Bank for Reconstruction and Development
ICASA	International Conference on AIDS and STIs in Africa (STIs—sexually transmitted infections)
ICSID	International Center for the Settlement of Investment Disputes
IDA	International Development Association
IEG	Independent Evaluation Group
IFC	International Finance Corporation
IFIs	international financial institutions
ILO	International Labour Organization
IMF	International Monetary Fund
IP	Inspection Panel
LICUS	low income countries under stress
MAP	Multicountry AIDS Program
MDGs	Millennium Development Goals
MDRI	Multilateral Debt Relief Initiative
MIGA	Multilateral Investment Guarantee Agency
NGO	nongovernmental organization
ODA	overseas development assistance
OECD	Organisation for Economic Co-operation and Development
PFP	policy framework paper
PRSP	poverty reduction strategy process
QAG	Quality Assurance Group
SDR	Special Drawing Rights
SWAP	sector wide approach
UNDP	United Nations Development Programme
UNESCO	United Nations Economic, Social and Cultural Organization
UNFPA	United Nations Population Fund
UNHCR	United Nations High Commissioner for Refugees
UNICEF	United Nations Children's Fund
WBI	World Bank Institute
WDR	World Development Report
WFDD	World Faiths Development Dialogue

Introduction

The World Bank today aspires to be the world's premier development institution. Its credo is captured by the bold phrase at the front entrance to its Washington, DC headquarters: "Our dream is a world free of poverty." The World Bank's central task is to work with the poorer countries of the world—some 100 today—to further their economic and social development. It does this by providing a combination of financial resources, technical support, advice and analysis, training, and coordination of development assistance. In practice the World Bank is deeply involved in virtually every facet of development, and is a major actor both in countries that seek its support and partnership and in the development community at large.

The World Bank is a specialized agency of the United Nations (UN), although it was created in 1944 before the 1945 founding of the UN, and for that reason sits somewhat apart within the UN system. Established at the same time as the International Monetary Fund (IMF), it sits across the street from the IMF;[1] the "Bretton Woods twins," as they are sometimes known, work together in a complex and evolving fashion, sometimes closely and in harmony, sometimes in tension as their styles and approaches are quite different.

Only a part of the World Bank's work happens at its large modern headquarters building, two blocks from the US White House. On any given day, several thousand teams are at work in over 120 countries, some based in the World Bank's many country offices, others traveling on what the Bank calls "missions." They work on a myriad of activities ranging from intense negotiations on urgent actions for a nation beset by financial crisis (with demonstrators clamoring for action on the streets), to routine discussions of economic data and options for reform; from field visits to remote agricultural sites, to knotty issues on purchasing pharmaceutical products or railway rolling stock; from conferences on sophisticated aspects of economic policy, to video consultations linking mayors from 20 countries; from encounters with civil society representatives about community engagement to discussions with educators about curriculum reforms.

No one person sitting in the headquarters building or working elsewhere grasps all the threads of activities bearing the label of the World Bank, so it is hardly surprising that the institution is generally poorly understood—and seen in very different lights from different perspectives. The World Bank consists of a complex set of multinational, multisectoral, multidisciplinary institutions that are involved in almost every aspect of development—which means, in practice, virtually every issue imaginable. The strength of the Bank lies in its capacity to span issues, sectors, and nations, to bring experienced professionals, ideas, networks, and finance to bear in advancing human welfare. Its challenges are to make this an effective and creative process; to achieve and be able to document development results; and to maintain and enhance its relevance in a dynamic world where private sector and other institutions are increasingly poised to play roles that the World Bank was created to play.

The World Bank has accumulated over six decades of experience. The institution's history parallels that of international relations and economic thought in the post-World War II era. Reflecting that history, the World Bank itself has changed dramatically over its lifetime, challenged and changed during each succeeding period.

The Bank began as a relatively minor player whose primary role was seen as financing postwar reconstruction in Europe and Asia. This intent was evident in the official and original title of the World Bank: the International Bank for Reconstruction and Development (IBRD). However, the US Marshall Plan soon assumed the role of rebuilding societies devastated by World War II, because the fledgling World Bank was neither financed nor organized to meet those needs. Over the succeeding decades, the second part of the institution's official title—development—became its core mission and *raison d'être* and the World Bank is today widely seen as the leading, though by no means sole, international development institution. The challenge of achieving equity in an unbalanced world is increasingly its challenge however, as it looks to the future.

So what is the World Bank? And why is its role often so difficult to explain? It helps, as a start, to acknowledge that the Bank is indeed a large and particularly complex entity. The World Bank is in fact made up of several quite distinct institutions which operate in different ways (see Box I.1). As a framework, let me introduce the World Bank by outlining four dimensions: (a) the World Bank is a cooperative, owned by its member governments; (b) it operates within and is shaped by the complex partnerships of contemporary development aid; (c) it is a financial organization that gives loans; and (d) as the Bank works with individual country governments, its programs differ widely from place to place.

The World Bank is a cooperative, owned in 2007, by 185 member countries. Their governments are the governors of the World Bank. They subscribe through a financial contribution and, based on the share in the Bank's capital, exercise voting rights; they exercise ultimate authority over the Bank's policies and operations. The Bank is not a cooperative in a legal sense (the term does not appear in its legal instruments), but the term conveys the aspirations and spirit of its governance. The aim is to act for the common good, to seek solutions that are beneficial to the collective, and to avoid controversies that divide or pit members one against one another. An important feature of the World Bank is that the voting shares are weighted by economic strength, and thus the governance structure is not designed to be democratic. This sets the World Bank apart from the rest of the UN system. Although wealthier countries clearly exercise greater power than lower-income countries, the organization strives to operate cooperatively, seeking consensus where possible.

The fact that the World Bank is a cooperative of member countries represented by their governments gives the institution an important character feature. Relationships are in the first instance with governments, and the Bank works to and through governments in its operations. This facet of the Bank's basic power structure is a given. While the Bank reaches out today far beyond public authorities, it is ultimately responsible to its governors, who represent governments, normally ministers of finance. Thus the World Bank is neither a private bank nor a private charity or foundation. It is indeed a public-sector institution, and its shareholders rarely allow its leaders to forget it, although this dynamic may not always be visible or evident to those who observe the Bank from outside.

Still, the World Bank now works as a partner in virtually every facet of its operations, as part of the multifaceted international development enterprise that has emerged over the past 40 years. This enterprise includes innumerable UN agencies, the aid agencies of national governments, regional and specialized multilateral development banks and agencies, nongovernmental organizations of every stripe, and private foundations, companies, and individuals. This maze is bewildering to all who must navigate it—not least leaders and civil servants in developing countries and social entrepreneurs with a vision for change.

The World Bank is often asked to play a guiding and coordinating role in this world of international economic affairs because it is a multilateral institution with broad and deep experience. Partnership arrangements take many different forms and the patterns are changing rapidly; it is a rare development activity—whether a study, a capacity-building exercise, or an investment—that does not involve several different institutions. It is no accident that a focus on achieving aid harmonization is one of the leading issues of the day within development circles.

The word "bank" in the World Bank's name also carries special significance. It links the institution's work and role to the world of finance and funding, and indeed many tend to regard the World Bank in the first instance as a source of money. Unlike many other organizations working in the development field, the World Bank has access to significant resources. The World Bank lends in the order of US$20–25 billion each year, and its outstanding loan and credit portfolio stood at $200 billion as of June 2007. Its approved operating budget for fiscal 2008 was $2.1 billion, and a myriad of other funds administered by the World Bank gave it still further financial leverage.

The financial character of the World Bank gives rise to several ironies and dilemmas. First, the identification of the World Bank with funding is often a problem in itself and can mislead many who frequently ignore or de-emphasize the important policy and intellectual roles. The financial independence of at least part of the World Bank's operations—those that involve lending, management of its assets, and borrowing on capital markets—does give it flexibility and leeway that many other development institutions lack. However, the "banking" role of the World Bank should not overshadow its many non-banking roles. Indeed, most who work at the World Bank understand well that money alone solves few problems, and that ideas are by far more important as a vector for lasting change. Lending and money are indeed central to the character and structure of the World Bank, but they are not the whole story.

Second, the Bank's relationships with developing countries often start and finish with financing as a central focus. The World Bank makes loans or offers concessional credits and grants, and in so doing exacts the financial discipline that goes with lending. It expects to be repaid. However, this financial diligence, which for many years lay at the heart of the Bank's strong reputation for probity and responsibility, evidently carries both benefits and drawbacks. Among the latter are rigidities that rendered it difficult to address the over-indebtedness of poor countries until a global citizens' movement (including Jubilee

2000) and ensuing action by the G-8 governments, nudged the development community towards new debt-relief mechanisms.

A third important characteristic of the World Bank is its strong country focus and character. The World Bank is a very different institution in different countries. This is usually appropriate, as the situations, needs, and policies of each country differ, and thus what they seek from their development partner also varies. A very poor country with severe budget constraints and lacking support and investment in many sectors (such as Mozambique in the early 1990s, just emerging from civil war and entirely dependent on external aid) has entirely different needs from a middle-income country like Brazil or Thailand. An agricultural economy with low primary school enrollment will similarly seek very different support from a transition economy in Eastern Europe. This much is fairly obvious.

However, this means that the World Bank operates with a very different style and with quite distinct means in Timor Leste, Indonesia, Vietnam, Cambodia, Zambia, Burkina Faso, Haiti, and Peru. Because the World Bank's relationships vary dramatically from country to country, so does the way the institution is seen and understood. The relationships between the World Bank and individual member countries—which sometimes carry five or six decades of history—also color what the Bank can and does do in important ways. In some countries, the Bank's influence is extraordinarily broad, extending to day-to-day issues and fundamental strategic choices. It can be a trusted advisor (the hoped-for model) or a stern arbiter. Yet in other countries, the Bank's role is far more limited, essentially a technical advisor in specific fields. The evolution of the Bank's role in China, its largest borrower over time, is an interesting illustration, as the Bank began there as a key advisor, privy to vital decisions involved in economic strategy and China's path in opening its economy to the world, yet the World Bank's role has evolved, with China's own development, into a sophisticated, and more technically driven role today.

While the World Bank has a large and complex array of global programs, because the World Bank's basic unit of account is the country, cross-country and regional operations are often difficult to pursue. In an era in which policies and speeches are woven through with references to globalization and transnational challenges, it is sometimes surprising how deeply the World Bank's country focus is engrained. There are important instances where the World Bank has engaged in regional operations but they involve special measures and lengthy negotiations and even so the country elements were still vital—examples include the World Bank's support for drought relief in the Sahel region in the 1970s, cross-border programs for HIV/AIDS in Africa, and tsunami relief in 2005.

This discussion so far has talked of the World Bank, but that masks yet another complexity of the institution: it is more accurate and informative to speak of the World Bank Group. The World Bank should be seen as composed of several different institutions, with different charters and mandates. The three principal institutions include the IBRD, also confusingly called the World Bank; the International Development Association (IDA), created in 1960 as a fund for concessional financing; and the International Finance Corporation (IFC), which lends to private companies for private-sector projects.

IBRD and IDA are tightly integrated and work as a single unit, though the financial terms associated with their lending to governments are very different. The IFC operates from a different building as a separate entity, with its own executive vice president, and its staff works with a different ethos, considering themselves more entrepreneurial than their "World Bank" colleagues. The World Bank Group also includes two other distinct though much smaller legal entities. The Multilateral Investment Guarantee Agency (MIGA) provides insurance to private companies against political risk, and the International Center for the Settlement of Investment Disputes (ICSID) completes the "World Bank Group." Box I.1 presents a schematic summary of these institutions.

Yet the five formal World Bank Group members are only part of the story and numerous other distinct institutions are housed within or near the World Bank. As examples, the Global Environment Facility (GEF) has an independent charter but works from the World Bank as does the Consultative Group to Assist the Poor (CGAP), the improbably named microfinance agency, which also operates as an autonomous entity based on a complex international partnership.

This brief account of the World Bank's multiple faces begins to explain the complex and sometimes contradictory roles that it is called upon to play and the controversies that surround it. It is positioned to be a visionary leader, with an unparalleled perspective on the global issues facing developing countries. It has close, daily ties with most if not all of its 185 member governments (and some beyond), and thus has a unique perspective on processes and issues related to public policy. The Bank is increasingly engaged on a wide range of global public issues with a wide range of public and private partners, companies, religious organizations, and nongovernmental organizations of all kinds. From this position it derives a coordinating role at both global and country levels. It is a knowledge institution, housing a highly educated staff, sitting on an extraordinary body of raw data and experience, and tapping a raft of relationships with universities and think tanks. The annual World Development Report explores leading development issues in a style that is professional and thorough, setting benchmarks for analysis and discussion for years to come.

Perceptions of the World Bank vary as widely as its different faces. It is broadly respected, and looked to for its resources, convening power, influence, and staff. The professionalism of its staff and its capacity for action, especially in times of crisis, are widely admired. The Bank is also vilified by significant groups as arrogant and narrowly focused; many have a critical view of its policies and operations, especially its slow engagement with environmental issues, its association with several unpalatable governments, and its economic advice (which, for example, has pressed reluctant governments toward sweeping macroeconomic and public sector reforms and privatization). The Bank's advice and financial support often come with elaborate and demanding strings attached, accentuating controversy and leaving long-lasting socio-political repercussions. Advocacy organizations have formed with the explicit objective of bringing the institution to a close and there is a large critical literature about World Bank operations. Many working in and with the Bank perceive it as a misunderstood institution. Critics call it a "one-eyed giant," a harsh but perceptive label that captures the institution's size and its tendency to view development primarily through the lens of economics (to the exclusion of other disciplines).[2] Above all, the World Bank is an important and powerful player in the critical challenges facing the world in fighting global poverty. If it did not exist, even critics agree, it would be necessary to create something similar. But the path that lies ahead for the World Bank is far from clear and smooth.

The following chapters explore the work of the World Bank through the dual lens of its practical, day-to-day work—largely in developing countries—and the debates that center on the institution's multiple roles, and the challenges its leaders face in navigating among them.

Chapter 1 elaborates the discussion here of the complex roles that the World Bank plays, and introduces the debates regarding its work. Because the World Bank is so central to the development world and profession, the chapter puts its work into a broader framework. How has understanding of what constitutes development taken shape? How have views about what "works" and what does not evolved? What role has the Bank been expected to play, how has it performed, and how can it continue to evolve?

Chapter 2 turns to a more specific account of the World Bank's history and evolution, and introduces the major elements of the organization and different parts of the World Bank Group. It takes a chronological approach, tackling the long and complex history of the World Bank which is the subject of several lengthy tomes, but seeks by that means to introduce major themes that have shaped that history.

Chapter 3 turns to nuts and bolts: what does a loan look like? What is the significance of a country strategy? How does the World Bank work with the UN Development Programme on the ground? The IMF? What does a consultative group do, and what mechanisms are in place to ensure that monitoring and evaluation occur, protect against corrupt use of funds, and report on the institution's work? Chapter 4 looks at the work of the World Bank from the perspective of the international development community, introducing some of the different players and the issues involved in the "aid business."

Chapter 5 looks at the practical side of the World Bank's work, relying on several specific cases to illustrate how the institution operates, and above all to show how staff confront analytical, practical, and ethical issues in the "real world." Chapter 6 returns to debates about the World Bank's role and explores why so much controversy surrounds the institution. It steps outside the Bank and presents the perspective of those who seek to change the institution, asking the question: what kind of institution would critics like to see, and what does that imply for the World Bank's future work?

Finally, Chapter 7 returns to the central issues under debate within the World Bank today that are likely to shape the institution's future: debts versus loans, focus on middle income or the poorest countries? How best to manage a complex knowledge institution in an increasingly dynamic and multipolar world? An appendix offers brief practical advice on working with the World Bank—what kinds of people work there, what kinds of questions to ask, and how to find answers.

This book is designed to help answer some questions about how the World Bank operates, painting a portrait of a complex institution full of idealistic pragmatists, of realistic idealists, an institution with noble intentions and practical tools, with features of a financial institution, a global think tank, and a part of the United Nations, with bad habits of obscure communication and a tendency to arrogance and slow processes, but deeply imbued with individual and collective determination to fulfill the "dream of a world without poverty."

Box I.1 Five institutions formally make up "the World Bank Group"

Thumbnail sketches follow of the organizations that formally constitute what is known as the World Bank Group. Terminology can be confusing as "the World Bank" often refers to the IBRD (in contrast to IDA), thus the "hard lending" institution, but it can also refer to IBRD and IDA together.

 International Bank for Reconstruction and Development (IBRD), also commonly known as the World Bank; established 1944, began operations 1946. Lends to creditworthy, thus middle income countries to support development and reconstruction.

 International Development Association (IDA), established in 1960, supports the development of the poorest countries with interest free loans (credits) or grants.

 International Finance Corporation (IFC), established in 1956, lends to and takes equity in private companies.

 International Centre for the Settlement of Investment Disputes (ICSID), established in 1966, provides facilities for the conciliation and arbitration of disputes between member countries and investors who qualify as nationals of other member countries.

 Multilateral Investment Guarantee Agency (MIGA), established in 1988, provides political risk insurance for foreign investments in developing countries, technical assistance to improve investment climates and promote investment opportunities in developing countries, and dispute mediation services, to remove possible obstacles to future investment.

1 "In the catbird's seat"
The World Bank and global development

The "catbird's seat" is a privileged place affording a unique vision and broad overview, as well as advantages of access. Though widely used, the derivation of "catbird's seat" is somewhat obscure. It refers to a bird that tends to sit at the highest point of a tree with the fullest view of its surroundings. The image describes well the World Bank's special position today in the world of international development.

The World Bank is one of many institutions working on development, but it is privileged by the unique breadth and depth of its perspective. It works at the highest levels of global and national leadership to help shed light on what is happening and envision what is coming. In the process, the World Bank has developed long and deep relationships—some enduring more than five decades—with most government ministries and institutions leading different sectors of national economies and societies, and is a key player in education, transport, power, health, and other vital arenas. The Bank has also often taken the lead in framing and addressing issues that cut across many sectors, including gender, the environment, and the climate for private investment.

And last but not least, the Bank works intensively to translate ideas and visions into reality—that is, to hammer out the overview and details of programs and budgets and monitor their execution. Through this work the Bank directly and constantly engages with communities and local institutions, and continuously gains extensive day-to-day practical experience.

No other organization operates in so many different domains. This puts the World Bank in a special position, well placed to see linkages and bring an informed and grounded perspective to bear. This engagement on many fronts is enhanced by the Bank's position as an international institution that, at least in theory, is removed from the hurly burly of national politics because it is an outside party and a respected international institution with a reputation for thorough analysis. And, with its international staff, it has the potential to bring widely different intellectual and cultural values to bear. Add to that the advantages of access that accompany the Bank's considerable resources—where money talks, the World Bank is heard. And when it is convinced to act (or allowed to do so by its governors), it can almost always mobilize the resources to support that action.

This unique position helps explain why the World Bank has so often played a central role on development issues as far afield as avian flu, global warming, clean water supplies, preschool education, and nutrition. It explains why the World Bank can continuously produce a remarkable array of analytic reports, why it so often chairs aid coordination groups for individual countries, why other analysts seek its views during economic crises, and why its processes for creating economic development and anti-poverty strategies often bring insight and solid information to discussions within individual countries and the aid community.

The World Bank's broad vision, however, carries some challenges, disadvantages, and risks. Because the Bank is involved in so many issues, the task of framing a strategic vision can, ironically, be particularly difficult. With so many threads, the possibility of bland rhetoric at one extreme or cacophony at the other is never far away. Many observers are uneasy with the multiplicity of tasks the contemporary World Bank pursues, and see a dispersion of effort. They argue for refocusing the Bank's mandate and mission on a narrower set of issues—for example economic issues and the classic work of infrastructure development. A different view (my own) is that the Bank's central challenge is to make the best of its privileged position, to bring very different perspectives together in creative ways, however demanding that may be. The Bank today is a highly interdisciplinary organization, with an ever-widening array of specialists. Extraordinarily complex teams are a hallmark of the World Bank's work, though fully integrating these different perspectives presents a constant challenge. When these assets are well employed, however, the Bank's insights are powerful.

Height confers advantages but also drawbacks. Because it operates at a global level, or at least with a broad vision, the World Bank often has difficulty both in seeing the individual trees in the forest and in linking its detailed work with the broader vision. Much of its work occurs within sectors, such as transport, education, or finance. Work within specific sectoral boundaries is well established and disciplinary focus within the traditional sectors is generally clear—for example, in education, with the respective roles of education economists, educators, and architects. When it comes to crosscutting issues, however, the bridges among sectors and disciplines may be harder to cross—say, the linkages between education programs, transport and health. This applies especially for the broad-brush analysis of global and national economic approaches and the far more specific micro-analysis resulting from project and sector work. The multitude of perspectives provided by day-to-day work at the local level can be hard to capture.

And with its privileged position come the dangers of arrogance and overconfidence in perspective and vision. The World Bank has not been known for its readiness to admit error or seek out opposing views. While this is changing, and many in the institution recognize the merits of humility, the stubborn image of arrogance is hard to shed. The potential for an inward-looking view is accentuated by the intrinsic difficulties in judging the impact of the Bank's work on development. The Bank is tackling some of the world's hardest issues and should be expected to fail in many of its efforts. Add to that that its role is almost always partial and indirect—it does not implement directly and is one of many players. The Bank too often fails to acknowledge both the intrinsic complexity and difficulty of its role and its own missteps and failures.

Investigating the multiple roles that the World Bank plays is key to understanding both its work and how it is perceived. But first it is important to appreciate how the hydra-headed institution of today has evolved, as its character is deeply embedded in its history. This chapter sketches how the very concept of development has taken shape and changed over the life of the World Bank (while the following chapter offers a more detailed account and analysis of the history itself). The common notion of development—and thus the job of the World Bank—was fundamentally different at the end of World War II, and has taken many turns since. This history explains much about shifts in the World Bank's work as a development institution over six decades.

A second important aspect reflects what many see as an important culminating point for ideas and action on international development: the formulation in the year 2000 of the Millennium Development Goals (MDGs). A review of how the World Bank fits into the architecture of the goals—in theory and in practice—is another important piece of the story of the World Bank's role in development.

Shaping development as a discipline and a mission

The term "development" is less straightforward than many would believe, and the very concept has changed radically over the past half-century.

When the World Bank was established, the concept of development was barely used in the contemporary sense. The responsibility of the global community and richer countries in addressing poverty and helping to assure an equitable path for all nations to develop their human and other resources was not defined. The name International Bank for Reconstruction and Development highlights that the development mission was understood at some level, but also that it clearly came second to reconstruction.

Visions of development that took shape in the early years after World War II were deeply influenced by the Cold War, which dominated approaches to international relations. These visions also shaped what was understood as a "just world" and how nations related to one another, as well as the role that was envisaged for the United Nations (UN) system. The polarized image of a "communist" path, associated with totalitarian governments and heavy state involvement in national economies, was contrasted with a model of freedom and market-led development. This polarization played out actively as many new nations became independent, especially in Africa. Each nation shaped its own vision of development, but these approaches were seen largely through the Cold War lens. Among the practical results of the polarization of views was the somewhat ironic juxtaposition of a generally suspicious approach among many World Bank managers and staff towards direct involvement in economic life by governments, seen as "socialist" in some lights, and an unease at direct confrontation about negative facets of socialist systems because this was seen as crossing the boundaries of "political interference." Blunter repercussions were the support that some leading World Bank member countries pressed for their "allied" countries, especially in Africa, even in the face of egregious economic and social management. The World Bank's continuing support for Zaire (now the Democratic Republic of the Congo) over the years and for Kenya and Zambia during turbulent periods, at the same time withholding support for countries like Albania and Vietnam, can be laid in part at the door of Cold War politics.

By the early 1960s, leading universities had established programs in development studies, analysts had written many books debating what worked and what did not, and the notion was taking root that richer countries had moral as well as practical obligations to help poorer countries catch up with their wealthier neighbors, through both policy-making and financing. But the notion of what it would take to achieve this catch-up was not clearly defined.[1]

The international financial institutions[2] clearly focused on investment, with a secondary emphasis on developing human resources (initially through technical assistance in economic management and project development and implementation, as well as training in a range of development skills, and later through increasing support for education policies and programs). But the overall vision was of a positive, relatively linear path of development. Most decision-making on funding for international development was confined to a narrow circle of policy-makers, as was implementation of specific programs. This picture started to change with the major droughts in Africa in the 1960s, but only in a few countries (the Scandinavian countries among them) did active debates of alternative paths and visions of development extend beyond small groups of academics and activists.

The 1970s and 1980s brought three major changes to this picture. The first was a steady broadening of the notion of development, which spurred institutions to recognize the complexity of the task confronting them. Education, health, nutrition, land tenure: a steady drumbeat of new topics appeared on agendas and filtered into organizations. The second, related, change was the emergence of doubts about how successful investments in infrastructure and human resources had been, especially but not solely in Africa. Major critiques began to suggest that all was not well behind the closed doors of the financial institutions. The rather complacent and confident tone of much development work began to give way to debates regarding how best to fulfill basic needs (a focus on providing the most essential services to people, like food, education, water, health) and integrated rural development (bringing together disparate programs and approaches so that there would be more coherence in efforts to support rural communities), among other concerns, and spawned a long series of new approaches and programs. The civil society revolution, which was to result in an explosion of institutions and movements over the last decades of the twentieth century, began to take shape and to seek admission into policy debates. And third, a string of economic crises—first in Latin America and then across Africa—had the effect of an electric shock, forcing practitioners and theorists to rethink basic concepts.

From a relatively self-confident and simplistic approach to development, the World Bank and institutions like it were slowly drawn into deeper reflection about what they were trying to do and what impact they had had. Evaluation emerged as a central theme: who would judge success, and how? Nongovernmental organizations and civil society institutions grew to parallel institutions like the World Bank, and the two camps began to encounter and engage each other, often through contention.

No issue exerted as much impact on development debates and visions as the environment. Development institutions at first viewed environmental critics as gnats annoying them with a buzz of critique, but gradually both the strength of their organizations and the merits of their arguments gained ground. The politics of these mushrooming critiques are a separate story, but a fundamental questioning of accepted concepts and basic values on environmental grounds caused seismic shifts over time and had broader repercussions; for example, it was the new safeguards on environment that, in many respects, opened the door to a far broader set of changes in social analysis. So, much more slowly, did changes in thinking about the roles of men and women. When it was first suggested, by critics and by people (especially women) within development institutions, that a special focus on issues for women was both essential and would strengthen development programs and their impact, the general response was (to say the least) skeptical, but over time a combination of evidence from research and operations and increasing voice of women began to shift the balance towards more openness. Gender strategies and analysis and probing questions about the impact of policies and programs on women came to be the norm. Today, many argue that the focus on women has become so much part of mainstream development thinking and practice that separate units and programs are hardly needed; this overstates progress but it is at least encouraging that in budget discussions it is now rare that gender programs are cited as the first on the list for cuts.

It began to dawn on many engaged in development work that the boundaries they had drawn around their mission and mandate—with parallel limits on ideas, policies, and procedures—had limited meaning, and were often quite flawed. A world neatly divided into first, second, and third worlds, development projects and economic advice, poor and rich, gave way to a far more complex picture.

The reflections about why many countries were not succeeding, why armed conflict seemed to persist and recur in some parts of the world, why so many carefully designed projects yielded disappointing results, and why technical assistance, provided at great cost and in staggering amounts, seemed still to leave yawning voids in capacity and continuing needs for outside advisors, led to much soul-searching. A healthy humility began to creep into some discussions, along with an appreciation of deep pathologies of development work, such as balkanization of projects by donor, and heavy-handed imposition of conditions and frameworks.

Two new mantras entered the discussion. The first was country ownership, reflecting the important observation that unless leaders and managers responsible for policies and programs are convinced and determined to act, development programs cannot succeed. Too often, it became clear, development institutions including the World Bank had taken too heavy a hand in program design, suiting it to their perceptions of how development should proceed, and had taken far too much at face value national government acceptance of proposed programs and conditions without testing commitment and recognizing the obvious pitfall that came when officials accepted proffered funds in the face of limited options. The second traced a path from consultation to participation and empowerment. This path reflected the crucial observation that communities must be far more directly involved in programs designed to help them. An array of advocacy, tools, and rules emerged to ensure that programs did indeed engage the people they most affected. Many civil society actors and local activists would fiercely contend that these insights were obvious from the start, but they were not part of mainstream development thinking until the 1990s.

The dawning appreciation of what actually happened at local levels, the reactions of individuals to development projects, and which incentives worked and which did not, paralleled growing awareness that information technology and transportation—the Internet, easier airline travel, the shift from mail to facsimile to email to cell phone—were spurring a revolutionary change in international relations. Some people describe globalization as a "project," but most have experienced it as something closer to a force of nature, bringing changes large and small, and forcing individuals and communities to reassess their identities, values, and relationships.

The globalization revolution became more widely apparent and began to shape views on development just as the fall of the Berlin Wall in 1989, the end of the Cold War, and the breakup of the former Soviet Union were also transforming international relations. The amazingly rapid realignment of state and global power politics exerted several immediate effects. First, many countries now sought support not for development, they said, but for transition. Second, shadow patronage of developing countries formerly tied to Cold War politics gave way to a complex and quite dynamic pattern of approaches among rich countries, which included changes in how they treated poorer nations. Nicaragua and Ethiopia, for example, had benefited from a protective attitude by the United States despite widely known and egregious corruption, but this shield was soon removed.

The new and multifaceted world of nation-states, and the stripping away of stylized, simplistic explanations which had implicitly underpinned at least some development thinking about what made countries rich and poor couched in terms of their political orientation (capitalist, socialist, communist), stimulated new thinking about the causes of poverty. It is hard to pinpoint a specific moment when a broad consensus took form around a global commitment to ending poverty, in part because the rhetoric about poverty and social justice has always been fulsome, even as practical engagement and action have been rather paltry. Nonetheless, the calls for action on poverty became increasingly urgent over time. A call to listen to the voices of the poor added another element to the debates—one that was far from academic and abstract. A more thoughtful appreciation of the depth of poverty, documented in many media and studies, helped spur a steep rise in activism, in turn facilitated by the information revolution and growth of democracy worldwide.[3] Among other topics, the heavy burden of poor-country debt galvanized many in poor and rich countries alike to protest not only specific debt policies that encouraged borrowing and made it extraordinarily difficult to reschedule or forgive unpayable debt burdens, but also the underlying economic, financial, and political models that had allowed debt to accumulate to patently unsustainable levels in the first place. Campaigns, including Jubilee 2000 helped to translate the long-standing and highly technical debate about debt policies into a widely comprehensible and compelling moral issue that engaged millions of citizens, crystallized much of the discontent, sparking alliances across widely different countries and interests.[4]

Many other historical events and forces also influenced thinking on development, including demographic changes which confounded planners of, for example, education facilities in many countries and generated a remarkable "youth bulge" that weighs heavily on job markets, skyrocketing urbanization which changes the face of countries, rising concerns about global warming which call traditional energy policies into question, and enormous changes in private capital flows and the structure of companies, multinational and international which have transformed understandings of what partnership is about. Growing support for human rights also shapes notions about what development involves, and how development should proceed—especially the obligations of different parties: development assistance is increasingly viewed not as voluntary charity fueled by compassion but as a matter of both basic justice and the common good. These important topics have shaped both the organization and the action of international development.

One megatrend bears special emphasis. The rise in international terrorist threats, especially the events of 11 September 2001, spurred much reflection about the links among poverty, instability, and extremism. Weak and failing states are now important concerns within the development community. A clear if unsurprising finding is that development programs work best in well-governed societies, so investing in weakly governed states is problematic. But how are weaker societies to become stronger if investment is curtailed? This reflection continues as weak states remain a leading strategic challenge of the early twenty-first century. The concept of human security, though used in different ways in different settings, at its core seeks to bring together the linked challenges of assuring physical security and safety with goals for a decent life for all, and builds on the insight that "shared security" for all people involves respecting their rights, their potential, and their different cultures and diversity, in short, working for greater equity and balance in the world.[5]

It is illustrative that the term "Third World" is still in use, although what is first and what is second is today quite obscure. One organization[6] refers to the "Two-Thirds World" to indicate that poor people and poor countries are the majority, despite their weaker power base. But the image of a complex mosaic is more apt. Country groupings based on income or even regional affiliations are in flux, and international relations are complicated. For example, China and India are both recipients of development assistance and important donors. The fates of several countries and their prospects have changed in a short time span, and intellectual structures that divide rich and poor, East and West, have less and less meaning. International programs at leading universities reflect this quicksand, as they try to define development and recognize that in practice it overlaps with other disciplines in countless ways, and that unique approaches to "developing countries" no longer make much sense. "Development" is not a separable field, but is so much part of international and domestic realities that it is misleading to treat it as a separate topic. The need for special focus on poverty and poor countries and to learn to navigate and work within the literature and institutions of development continues to be critically important, but these topics need to be an integral part of research and teaching across disciplines, rather than the "ghetto" it was threatening to become some years ago.

Shifts in development theory and approaches—which in turn shape and have been shaped by the World Bank—are thus intricately woven into the history of the post-World War II world. It should hardly be surprising, therefore, that different actors see this history in radically different ways, and that views are far from unanimously held. Ensuing chapters will explore how these differing perspectives play out in relation to the World Bank and its work.

Millennium challenges and the World Bank

The MDGs were born of the extraordinary reflections inspired by the approaching turn of the century in 2000. Looking back on numerous global meetings of the previous decades, many perceived rather paltry results. Looking beyond those meetings to the "state of the world," many saw billions of people still living lives of poverty and suffering, despite ardent promises and an array of aid programs. The world's global institutions and their leaders as well as nongovernmental organizations and civic activists looked for new formulas.

Heads of state attending the Millennium Summit at the UN in September 2000 agreed to work more effectively, and together, to bring poverty to an end. And facing more skepticism than ever about the rhetoric that inevitably emerges from international meetings, UN institutions framed the summit's promises in terms of specific goals and targets, with dates, quantitative indicators, and an allocation (at least in a notional form—for example highlighting roles of developing nations to assure good governance and of wealthier nations to assure adequate funding) of responsibility for implementation. By 2015, the world will halve poverty, end hunger, and ensure that all children finish primary school, among other goals. The MDG framework is designed to serve as a map and provide a set of benchmarks for all global institutions (see Box 1.1 and the elaborate MDG web site[7]).

Box 1.1 The Millennium Development Goals[8]

1 Eradicate extreme poverty and hunger
   - Reduce by half the proportion of people living on less than a dollar a day
   - Reduce by half the number of people who suffer from hunger

2 Achieve universal primary education
   - Ensure that all boys and girls complete a full course of primary schooling

3 Promote gender equality and empower women
   - Eliminate gender disparity in primary and secondary education preferably by 2005 and at all levels by 2015

4 Reduce child mortality
   - Reduce by two thirds the mortality rate among children under five

5 Improve maternal health
  - Reduce by three quarters the maternal mortality ratio

6 Combat HIV/AIDS, malaria and other diseases
  - Halt and begin to reverse the spread of HIV/AIDS
  - Halt and begin to reverse the incidence of malaria and other major diseases

7 Ensure environmental sustainability
  - Integrate the principles of sustainable development into country policies and programs; reverse loss of environmental resources
  - Reduce by half the proportion of people without access to safe drinking water
  - Achieve significant improvement in lives of at least 100 million slum dwellers, by 2020

8 Develop a global partnership for development
  - Develop further an open trading and financial system that is rule based, predictable and non-discriminatory, includes a commitment to good governance, development and poverty reduction—nationally and internationally
  - Address the least developed countries' special needs. This includes tariff- and quota-free access for their exports; enhanced debt relief for heavily indebted poor countries; cancellation of official bilateral debt; and more generous official development assistance for countries committed to poverty reduction
  - Address the special needs of landlocked and small island-developing States
  - Deal comprehensively with developing countries' debt problems through national and international measures to make debt sustainable in the long term
  - In cooperation with the developing countries, develop decent and productive work for youth
  - In cooperation with pharmaceutical companies, provide access to affordable essential drugs in developing countries
  - In cooperation with the private sector, make available the benefits of new technologies—especially information and communications technologies

The World Bank has been and remains very much part of the MDG process. Apart from providing specific comments on the goals and targets at global, regional, and country levels, the World Bank was asked specifically to contribute an important element: a price-tag. What would it cost to achieve the goals, and how could the cost be financed? The desire to make the goals and targets concrete was behind a second milestone: a conference on Financing for Development held in Monterrey, Mexico, in March 2002. Despite the pall cast by 11 September 2001, the Monterrey conference seemed a defining moment when a global consensus and collective determination to work to end poverty became clear. As James D. Wolfensohn, president of the World Bank, was fond of saying, every leader had signed off on the MDGs and there was "no place to hide."

The year 2005 was seen as the first major checkpoint between 2000 and 2015, and it brought intensive reviews and mobilization, culminating in the G-8 meeting at Gleneagles, Scotland, in July 2005. The overall diagnosis was not favorable. Many individual countries, and especially a major region, Africa, were not on track to achieve the goals. Leaders from all across the world, including the World Bank, rededicated themselves to working in a new partnership to achieve the MDGs. Preparations for a next milestone in 2010 are underway, all with a view to the specific time target for the MDGs: 2015.

Thus the MDG framework today represents the closest the international community has come to reaching consensus on the meaning of development, priorities for action, and responsibilities for implementation. The MDGs are far from perfect. They are not comprehensive, they are framed in very general terms, they are in some sense very limited (some groups call them the Minimum Development Goals), and an elaborate structure designed to facilitate quantitative monitoring also imposes a certain rigidity. However, if they are used as a map and not a blueprint, if they are translated into images with human content, the MDGs can indeed be a force for good, a framework that can guide the international development world as it moves forward.

Beyond the details of the targets and goals, the MDG compact reflects an important and inspirational new vision of what development is about. Over the remarkable era following World War II, woven through momentous political and social transformations, two related concepts took root. The first was that poverty and misery were not inevitable, and that economic and social progress was possible and desirable for all nations. Second, the developed world has a responsibility to support this process with resources and leadership. This is the vision that inspires the best of the leadership and approach of the World Bank today, and that lies behind the statement by its front door: "Our dream is a world free of poverty."

Thus the development world has undergone its own revolution, evolving from a quiet, often deliberate, and technically driven effort led by a few economists and institutions based in the wealthiest countries to a fast-paced multinational and multisectoral world with countless actors holding very different ideas about what works and what does not. Changes in the priorities and practices of the World Bank—explored in the next chapter—reflect this fundamental transformation in thinking about development during its lifetime.

Summary

The World Bank, among development institutions, is privileged by its global reach, multilateral character, access to resources, and breadth of activity. This explains both the central role it plays on development issues as different as avian flu, global warming, clean water supplies, preschool education, and nutrition, and also, to a degree, the lightening rod of controversy it attracts. The Bank's privileged position carries challenges, disadvantages, and risks, including tendencies to arrogance, imperviousness to different voices, and spreading its resources too thin. The complex roles the World Bank plays have been shaped by sweeping changes in the very concepts of what development is about over the past six decades, simplistic visions of a linear orderly process in a polarized world giving way to a far richer, more nuanced appreciation of the enormous diversity of development paths, the importance of different cultures, and an explosion of development actors. Today leading development issues include approaches to weak and failing states, effective approaches to rights and equity, and the practical meaning of human security. The historic definition by the world's leaders and nations of concretely defined goals and targets for development (the MDGs) following the 2000 UN Millennium Summit provide a framework encouraging action, integrated action, and accountability for results. It is within this broad and fast-changing context that the World Bank has evolved and in which its future will be shaped.

2 How the World Bank has evolved in response to global events

The World Bank of 2007 is a far different institution from that envisaged by its founders in the mid-1940s. Its basic objectives have evolved from a relatively straightforward focus on financing reconstruction to aspirations to act and speak for the poorest segments of society worldwide. Its operations today are also vastly different in scope, nature, and geography, as are its size and prominence. As the balance of global power has shifted, so have the Bank's relationships with national governments, international institutions, civil society and the private sector.

Indeed, the World Bank has proved remarkably durable and adaptable, changing perhaps rather slowly but nonetheless profoundly in response to world events and its own experience. Whether it has adapted sufficiently—whether it is equipped to meet the challenges of the current era—is a question for a subsequent chapter. This chapter traces the intricate history of the World Bank as it has responded to profound new problems, and as it has contributed to the emergence of the "development business" and the twenty-first-century focus on creating a more just and equitable world.

An important objective behind the creation of the World Bank was to finance the immense reconstruction needs of the post-World War II world. However, while the World Bank remains an important actor in various types of reconstruction after wars, economic crises, and natural disasters, its primary focus shifted early on toward economic and social development.

As the meaning of "development" deepened from a somewhat shadowy and poorly elaborated notion of progress to a complex and heavily debated set of approaches today, the World Bank itself took on a far more central role. The Bank also began to focus more intensely on the poorest countries, and the poorest communities within those countries—with fighting poverty increasingly seen as its overarching mission.

Today the World Bank is widely regarded as a leading voice supporting the economic and social development of poor nations. The Bank's antipoverty work has spurred it to grapple with the complex notion of equity, which includes human welfare, prosperity, and quality of life as well as income distribution and human rights (though this is rarely mentioned frontally, the issues that underlie human rights concerns are much in discussion within the World Bank). The contemporary World Bank is thus deeply engaged in all three challenges: reconstruction, development, and equity.

The World Bank's evolution reflects tumultuous historical developments. These include not only the deeply divided ideologies and strategic alliances of the Cold War and the end of colonialism as a major force, but also diverging regional development patterns, tensions around US domination after the Cold War, and the fast-paced and profound social, economic and technology changes of the globalization era. The profound changes in the array of global institutions such as the United Nations (UN) system and private-sector and civil society groups have also vigorously shaped the Bank's role. Theories about economic and social change, too, have shifted radically during the World Bank's lifetime and shaped its course—even as the Bank itself has shaped those ideas. And the Bank's own lived experience in managing and funding thousands of projects in well over 130 countries has given the institution its form today.

The intent and creation[1]

The overall design for the new World Bank played out during debates near the end of World War II and before the creation of the UN, largely within a small circle of financial officials and commentators. The Bretton Woods institutions—as the World Bank and the International Monetary Fund (IMF) are often called because of their joint birth at the July 1944 conference of representatives of 44 countries at the mountain resort in Bretton Woods, New Hampshire—were largely the brainchild of financial leaders in the US government, with the United Kingdom (especially economist John Maynard Keynes) taking an active part in the final discussions.

These leaders regarded the IMF and the International Bank for Reconstruction and Development (IBRD) as key components of the postwar global architecture, designed to prevent the kind of financial vicissitudes they saw as major causes of the tensions that produced World War II, and providing the scaffolding for sound financial relationships among nations. The thinking behind the IMF at the time was far more elaborate—indeed, the World Bank was in some respects an afterthought. Nonetheless, the joint birth of the Bretton Woods twins was reflected in their linked missions and parallel governance framework. A particularly relevant proviso is that membership in the World Bank is conditional on membership in the IMF, and the IMF quota which determines share capital subscription rights and thus voting power also drives a country's contribution rights to shares and thus power within the World Bank.

The Articles of Agreement for the IBRD—accepted by the participants at Bretton Woods, and ratified by the requisite number of nations by the end of 1945—provide the basic governance structure that guides the institution today. Though the world and the institution have changed radically, the enduring bones of these articles are thus worth highlighting. President Roosevelt's message to Congress on the legislation authorizing the IMF and IBRD gives some insight into the spirit and intent of its founders (see Box 2.1).

Box 2.1 President Franklin D. Roosevelt's message to Congress on the Bretton Woods money and banking proposals

I said before, and I repeat again: "This generation has a rendezvous with destiny."

If we are to measure up to the task of peace with the same stature as we have measured up to the task of war, we must see that the institutions of peace rest firmly on the solid foundations of international political and economic cooperation. The cornerstone for international political cooperation is the Dumbarton Oaks proposal for a permanent United Nations.

International political relations will be friendly and constructive, however, only if solutions are found to the difficult economic problems we face today. The cornerstone for international economic cooperation is the Bretton Woods proposals for an international monetary fund and an international bank for reconstruction and development. . . .

The main job of restoration is not one of relief. It is one of reconstruction which must largely be done by local people and their Governments. They will provide the labor, the local money and most of the materials. The same is true for all the many plans for the improvement of transportation, agriculture, industry and housing, that are essential to the development of the economically backward areas of the world.

They should help the countries concerned to get production started, to get over the first crisis of disorganization and fear, to begin the work of reconstruction and development; and they should help our farmers and our industries to get over the crisis of reconversion by making a large volume of export business possible in the post-war years.

Almost no one in the modern world produces what he eats and wears and lives in. It is only by the division of labor among people and among geographic areas, with all their varied resources, and by the increased all-around production which specialization makes possible, that any modern country can sustain its present population. It is through exchange and trade that efficient production in large units becomes possible. To expand the trading circle, to make it richer, more competitive, more varied, is a fundamental contribution to everybody's wealth and welfare.

It is time for the United States to take the lead in establishing the principle of economic cooperation as the foundation for expanded world trade. We propose to do this, not by setting up a super-government, but by international negotiation and agreement, directed to the improvement of the monetary institutions of the world and of the laws that govern trade.

Franklin D. Roosevelt, the White House, February 12, 1945

The core belief was that the World Bank (as the IBRD came to be known almost from the very start) would spur reconstruction and development by catalyzing private-sector investment. Although the private sector would be the motor for economic growth, the World Bank would facilitate its work by financing specific public-sector projects to remove bottlenecks, where appropriate. Nowhere do the articles specify that the World Bank will work only in poorer countries— indeed, it operated in several distinctly non-poor countries like Australia and Japan until 1967—nor is fighting, much less ending, poverty, defined as a priority. Also noteworthy is the absence of any conception of divisions among "first, second, and third" worlds, as the coming Cold War was not apparent in 1944. Moreover, the articles do not articulate either a framework for development or a specific approach, nor do they define "project" precisely, though they clearly indicate a bias toward project lending.

However, the Bretton Woods founders did define two lasting characteristics of the institution. First, the articles prohibit the Bank from political involvement, a proviso triggered primarily as a response to concerns about potential ideological clashes involving the Soviet Union (which participated at Bretton Woods but then did not ratify the articles):

> The Bank and its officers shall not interfere in the political affairs of any member; nor shall they be influenced in their decisions by the political character of the member or members concerned. Only economic considerations shall be relevant to their decisions, and these considerations shall be weighted impartially in order to achieve the purposes stated in Article I.[2]

The second core characteristic of the Bank was the design of voting rights and governance. The articles indelibly established the principle of one governor per member country. However, voting power is determined by each country's share of World Bank capital—which in turn reflects that country's economic strength. Thus power is heavily weighted toward wealthier countries, especially the United States, the largest shareholder. The articles also delegate much of the governors' power to an executive board, and to a president appointed by the board.

The most significant public debates during the ratification stages for the articles of agreement took place as part of the authorization process in the US Congress and centered on the IMF. The World Bank emerged from the process largely undebated and unscathed.[3] The World Bank was officially ready for business on 31 December 1945.

From reconstruction to development

The early years of the World Bank saw an uneasy and rather slow start to operations and a major shift in its mandate from reconstruction to development. These years also saw the creation of the UN, and a working out of relations between the World Bank and the UN and its specialized agencies.

Although the founding of the World Bank had appeared to proceed rather harmoniously, hitherto hidden minefields and outright disagreements became apparent when the board of governors first met in Savannah, Georgia, in March 1946. Two topics that would cast long

and enduring shadows sparked sharp debate there: the physical location of the World Bank, and the role and remuneration of the executive board. The articles had specified that the Bank would be located
with the largest shareholder, thus the United States—but the question
remained whether the headquarters should be in New York or
Washington, DC.[4] The decision, to the unhappiness of several members, went in favor of Washington, thus ensuring a marked tendency
towards active links between the Bank and the US government, and,
more broadly, affirming the importance of relationships with public
authorities (versus private markets). The United States also favored a
permanent and well-paid executive board, to ensure an active and
professional role for directors and continuing links to shareholder
governments, and again won out over objections, especially from the
UK. The World Bank (like its twin, the IMF) would thus have the
unusual feature of a permanent, resident, salaried board of directors,
who would inevitably engage directly in many facets of the institution's work.

These governance arrangements laid the foundation for another
enduring characteristic: the strong role of the World Bank's president.
The articles do not specify the nationality of the president, nor elaborate on the appointment process (except to specify that the board
appoints the president).[5] However, the president was without dispute
expected to be an American in the early years, though from the 1970s
there was at least debate as to whether the US President should be
entitled to a unilateral nomination; the practice has persisted largely
because it forms part of a broader informal agreement that gives
Europeans the right to nominate the Managing Director of the IMF
and developing countries the UN Secretary-General. In 1946, therefore, the selection process played out within the United States, directly
engaging President Truman (without congressional approval, as the
Bank president is an international civil servant). In June 1946, after
several false starts and delays, Eugene Meyer, a respected leader and
publisher of the *Washington Post*, agreed to take on the presidency
(several men had turned it down, and he was initially reluctant), and
the Bank started operations later that very month. Meyer's brief (six-
month) tenure was not a happy one, dominated by struggles with the
board, but the Bank nonetheless began to consider loan applications
during this period, focusing on Europe.

Meyer's immediate successor (as acting president), Harold Smith,
died within weeks of taking the post. The next presidential appointment was far happier, after John McCloy became president in March
1947. A magnetic personality, a lawyer with good private-sector contacts,

he and his vice president, Robert Garner, started to put the World Bank on its feet. Their clear immediate priority was Europe's reconstruction. Within two months, the Bank had approved a $250 million loan for France, followed by a $195 million loan to the Netherlands in August 1947, and shortly afterward loans for $40 million to Denmark and $12 million to Luxembourg.

However, the postwar reconstruction challenges were soon recognized to be vastly greater and more urgent than the fledgling institution was in any position to meet. Further, the Bank's financing structure was still provisional, untested, and heavily dependent on the capital the US had paid in dollars; the institution had no operating procedures and only a small staff. These circumstances led the US government to rethink its approach to reconstruction, and to design a US-led and US-financed process that left the World Bank entirely to the side. Secretary of State George C. Marshall announced the Marshall Plan (or the European Recovery Program, as it was formally known) in June 1947 in an address at Harvard University, and it immediately became the focus and fulcrum for reconstruction. Although the World Bank continued to consider several pending applications for reconstruction loans, its focus quickly shifted to the second, hitherto neglected, part of its mandate: development (although its reconstruction role later reappeared as an important part of its business). The Bank made its first development loan to Chile, for $16 million for agricultural machinery in March 1948, followed by loans to Mexico and Brazil in early 1949.

Building a reputable bank

The World Bank came into being with a limited financial plan and restricted resources, and without specific procedures or clear precedents for lending. The remarkable achievement of the decade and a half from the late 1940s to 1960 was the creation of a widely respected lending institution with a well-understood role, a solid financial reputation, access to private financial resources, a professional and highly regarded staff, and a battery of procedures to guide its lending operations.

The financial structure of the World Bank has several complex and unique aspects, and not surprisingly these have changed over the years as the institution has grown and the international financial world has been transformed. To simplify, the initial and broad financial structure envisaged an institution that relied on capital—initially totaling $10 billion—subscribed (that is, committed as equity) by all members in proportion to their financial capacity. Nations would actually pay in only part of what they had promised (20 percent initially), with the remainder "callable" under undefined circumstances. The IBRD expected to fund its operations largely by borrowing on private markets. Because the cost of borrowing these funds determined the interest rates the IBRD would charge its borrowers, the IBRD loaned funds at close to commercial terms despite the subsidy provided by the financial architecture of IBRD.[6]

The IBRD's financial architecture and the need to enter private financial markets required a courtship with Wall Street—in the late 1940s the primary if not the only place to search for funds. Making this structure work required some time, especially to establish a reputation that promised reliable servicing of debt and prudent stewardship of finance, the key to assuring reasonable borrowing and lending costs. Attentive cultivation of relationships with private markets was thus a high early priority for the Bank's leaders, and they proved remarkably adroit in this process. A first bond offering in July 1947 for $250 million was successful, and this was a source of relief and gratification.[7] The World Bank had both some resources to work with and the beginnings of a reputation, which it has nurtured and developed with great care over the decades. The triple-A bond rating that the Bank earned in 1959 has never been in question, and counts as an enduring asset and achievement.

The Bank's early loans sparked considerable debate, as another lingering cloudy area was the "project" focus of lending explicitly required by the articles, and how often "exceptional circumstances" allowed by the articles could apply. The former provision reflected a determination by the founders to lend only for clearly defined investments, to avoid the loose financing seen as a major contributor to the financial interwar catastrophe. However, the Bank's earliest loans—for reconstruction in Europe—clearly fell into the "exceptional" category as finance was not allocated to any specific investments, raising continuing questions as to when, whether, and under what conditions the Bank could and should provide loans for more general development programs "in exceptional circumstances." Still, the bias in the early years, with the notable exception of lending to Europe, was toward investing in projects, meaning well-defined activities where the use of funds was clearly detailed.

This focus shaped the core discipline of appraising potential projects, helping to prepare them (as full-blown project proposals failed to arrive at the Bank's door), and helping to speed their implementation. Bank officials also developed procedures for procurement, accounting, and project supervision, as well as requirements for managing projects. Here again the World Bank was defining new paths, and it gained a reputation for prudence, careful appraisal techniques, and pragmatic methodologies that stood the test of time.

Early expectations were that the lending process would be fairly simple, with countries submitting loan applications and the World Bank assessing their viability. However, in practice the Bank found itself in the business of helping shape project proposals and, from the start, it saw itself as having responsibilities for judging how well projects fit country circumstances, and how much they would contribute to a country's economic progress. Early operational work also drew attention to the importance of managerial skills: development was not simply about financing but involved the full battery of disciplines and skills needed to make projects work. Training administrators in developing countries thus quickly became an important Bank activity.

Infrastructure was the main focus of lending during the early years: well over half of all loans financed electric power, transportation, and water supply projects. This thrust reflected the idea that the Bank's role was to support the infrastructure that would allow private investment to flourish, as well as its early emphasis on ensuring financial returns so that the project's revenues would directly assure repayment of the loan. Only gradually, beginning in the 1960s, did the World Bank's notions of development and its own operations broaden and deepen—notably with the 1963 addition of lending for education, and progressive extension to other sectors. The expectation of a direct link between a loan and capacity to repay by the entity concerned gave way to an understanding of government responsibility for servicing debt where a broader public interest was served which opened the door to very different conceptions of projects and appropriate sectors for World Bank support.

The central role of the World Bank president took shape in the early years with a succession of strong leaders, each of whom gave the World Bank a marked and highly personal imprint. When John McCloy, the World Bank's second president, resigned in May 1949, he was succeeded by Eugene Black, a former banker, who had served as the US executive director for the Bank, and who became its longest-serving president, from 1949 until 1963. He was succeeded by George D. Woods, who was president until April 1968. Robert S. McNamara then became president, also serving for a lengthy period (13 years), and putting perhaps the strongest personal stamp on the institution of any of its presidents to date. Box 2.2 gives a quick summary of succeeding World Bank presidents.

Box 2.2   Presidents of the World Bank

Robert Zoellick (July 2007–?)

Paul Wolfowitz (June 2005–2007)

Served as president, following a career in the US government and academia, during a turbulent period, reaffirmed priority of the World Bank role on Africa, importance of fighting corruption.

James D. Wolfensohn (June 1995–June 2005)

Known as the "Renaissance Banker." Pushed through reforms that have made the Bank more inclusive, with a renewed focus on poverty reduction.

Lewis Preston (September 1991–May 1995)

Distinguished commercial banker. Helped foster a client-oriented vision for the Bank as it celebrated its fiftieth anniversary.

Barber Conable (July 1986–August 1991)

Spurred on the "greening" of the Bank, promoted focus on gender and development, oversaw major reorganization to promote country focus.

Alden Winship Clausen (July 1981–June 1986)

Improved the financial management of the Bank. Wrestled with the onset of recession and the 1980s debt.

Robert Strange McNamara (April 1968–June 1981)

Expansionist with a social consciousness tireless leader who increased both the size and visibility of the World Bank in many areas.

George David Woods (January 1963–March 1968)

"...credited with a great vision for the Bank and a number of bold innovations." (The World Bank: Its First Half Century, Brookings Institution, 1997.)

Eugene Robert Black (July 1949–December 1962)

Built a solid financial foundation and led the Bank into an era of financial diplomacy. Much-admired chairman of the Board and popular CEO.

John Jay McCloy (March 1947–June 1949)

Launched the Bank in business and lifted its vision from reconstruction to development.

Eugene Meyer (June 1946–December 1946)

Laid the groundwork for lasting Bank business policies.

Creating mechanisms for private investment

A seminal marker was the establishment in 1956 of the World Bank's first major affiliate: the International Finance Corporation, or IFC. From the Bank's earliest days, its leaders and key observers had concluded that its overall plan had an important missing link: it was unable to lend directly to private companies, buy equity in them, or help manage them. Yet the fundamental idea was that the World Bank should play a catalytic role *vis-à-vis* the private sector. IFC took shape after a series of studies, some by the UN, highlighted the need for a mechanism to support private investment, and then through negotiations on its own Articles of Agreement. The articles gave the new institution considerable autonomy within the ambit of the World Bank, with its own staff, executive director, and limited authorized capital.

IFC began operations promptly in 1956, but its start was rather slow. It faced a fundamental Catch-22 trap well into the 1970s. Its mandate was to finance projects that were inherently risky—those in which private parties would not invest without IFC's imprimatur—yet that were also profitable and sound enough to justify IFC's prudent investment. IFC thus developed rather deliberately as it navigated these shoals, but gradually took on a clear institutional ethos as the private-sector arm of the World Bank Group. In its first five years, IFC made 45 investment commitments totaling $58 million, while over the next five years its investments averaged $20 million annually.

IFC was by no means the only part of the World Bank that engaged private companies; a broad focus on the private investment climate was a strong thread running through the Bank's approach from the start. However, this concern brought the Bank into early tension with the proviso that it should not interfere in the political affairs of member countries. For example, the Bank was reluctant to lend to nations that had unpaid public-sector debt (the Bank then viewed failure to service debt as basically immoral), that allowed state-owned enterprises to play too large a role, and that had expropriated private property without compensation. Many early discussions within the World Bank and up and down decisions on loan applications turned on these issues.

Although early thinking had envisaged the Bank as offering guarantees for private lending for projects, these instruments did not prove practical right away. Still, they remained a subject of discussion, and the Bank approved several guarantees in the mid-1980s. The major step came in 1988 with the creation of the Multilateral Investment

Guarantee Agency (MIGA), designed to insure private investors against political risk and provide technical assistance and dispute mediation involving governments and private investors. Working as an integral part of the World Bank Group but with considerable autonomy, MIGA began operations slowly but picked up steam in the 1990s. By 2007 the organization had grown to a staff of around 100, and had approved 850 guarantees in 92 countries for projects worth more than $17 billion.

Established a place in the United Nations system

Although both the World Bank Articles of Agreement and the UN Charter had anticipated that the two would form part of a single system, working out the details of relationships took time and was not easy. The fledgling UN had expected and hoped that the World Bank and IMF would in effect report to it, while leaders of the Bretton Woods institutions had no such intention. After several rounds of rather tense discussions, these leaders reached a formal agreement in November 1947 making the World Bank and the IMF specialized agencies of the UN. However, they were and have remained "rather 'special' specialized agencies."[8] The clear intention of the World Bank and the IMF to maintain their financial autonomy gave rise to complex arrangements for coordinating the work of both institutions with the UN system. For example, the Bretton Woods institutions report annually to the UN Economic and Social Council (ECOSOC) and participate in many UN meetings.

The World Bank has also developed cooperative arrangements with specialized UN agencies—most importantly with the UN Development Programme (UNDP) which also exercises a lead role within the UN for development work. Important formal cooperative arrangements with the Food and Agriculture Organization, and the United Nations Education, Scientific, and Cultural Organization (UNESCO) have brought the institutions into close and regular contact. The Bank also has developed close partnerships with other UN-specialized institutions, notably the United Nations Children's Fund (UNICEF), the UN High Commissioner for Refugees, and the United Nations Population Fund. However, it is not beholden to the UN for approval of its policies and actions and above all for financial support. The fundamental difference in governance structures gives the World Bank (and the IMF) a special status within the UN system, a status that is subject to continuing debate and not insignificant tensions, especially when directly or indirectly political issues come into the arena.

The postcolonial world transformed

The World Bank early on made no bones about the fact that it was a bank. It expected to lend, it led with lending, and it expected to be repaid. Its officers had little sympathy with talk of grants, and far less with rescheduling debt. The predominant belief was that the key gap (which had in fact been a major practical constraint for early Bank operations) was a lack of well-prepared projects, and a related lack of management skills and weak institutions. The latter diagnoses took the World Bank into the world of technical assistance, which became a major focus. It was also drawn into analyzing each country's situation and prospects through economic reports, which tended to be meticulously prepared, multivolume works.

This ordered vision of the world and the Bank's role within it progressively eroded as the year 1960 approached. Decolonization was proceeding far more rapidly than the Bank's founders had anticipated, and it was becoming crystal clear that the resulting new nations—especially but not exclusively in Africa—were not creditworthy on the near-commercial terms at which the Bank's financial structure allowed it to lend. Discussions and preparatory work within the US government, the UN, and the World Bank itself since the mid-1950s had focused on the significant financial needs of these new nations. Especially within the UN, passionate discussions highlighted the need to ensure adequate finance for these nations' development, and a variety of abortive proposals for special funds were considered and foundered. However, these discussions ultimately gave rise to a new entity of the World Bank Group: the International Development Agency, or IDA, whose Articles of Agreement were approved in 1960.

Unlike IBRD, IDA depends on grant contributions from wealthier nations—set initially at a total of $1 billion—which the agency lends to poorer nations on highly concessional terms. The management of this system and its overall operating policies would mimic those of IBRD, which would run the new fund. Bank historians have referred to this arrangement as "an elaborate fiction"[9] because IDA appears to be a separate entity, while the reality is that it functions as an integral part of the Bank, often so closely allied that the two are indistinguishable except in financial structure and financial terms. Still, that distinction is an important one. The IBRD relies on careful tests of creditworthiness to determine whether a country is eligible and for what amount before lending on close to commercial terms. IDA, in contrast, offers "credits" (distinct from IBRD loans) with 0 percent interest, repayment over 40 years after a 10-year grace period, and a

0.75 percent service charge on outstanding amounts. These terms have hardened somewhat since 1987, with the overall term now 40 years in countries with loans from IDA only, and 35 years in countries with loans from both IBRD and IDA. IDA grants were introduced in 2002 for some IDA countries and projects.

Through the elaborate and often protracted series of negotiations with member governments that led to successive new financing agreements (termed "replenishments"), as well as specific IDA experience which was concentrated in the poorest countries, a distinct set of IDA issues and priorities took shape over time. Given the complex symbiotic relationship between IDA and IBRD, IDA was instrumental in shaping the approach and ethos of the World Bank overall (and vice versa). Nonetheless several well-defined IDA principles have emerged, largely as a response to competition among poor nations for the IDA's limited funds available on highly concessional terms.

When the need for mechanisms for allocating IDA credits became obvious, the first criterion that emerged was a country's overall poverty level. While IDA awarded early credits to more prosperous countries because they could develop and propose projects more quickly, consensus quickly arose that the poorest countries should have priority, and IDA governors established clear income ceilings on eligibility. A country's performance on earlier projects was also an important criterion, which became more feasible to apply with IDA's growing experience. Because India and Pakistan could dwarf other countries if per capita allocations were the benchmark, given their large populations, a weighting to ensure allocation to all countries emerged. Thus poverty, performance, and population became the key criteria for allocating credits.

IDA negotiators had explored the types of projects that should receive funding, and expected the organization to back those with more social objectives than the standard infrastructure fare of the IBRD of the day. Indeed, IDA's openness to financing education projects bumped IBRD into that field. Supporters also expected that IDA would, like IBRD, normally finance specific projects. However, an "escape clause" again allowed for exceptional circumstances, and in practice IDA's early lending helped on a regular basis to finance general imports in support of the development plans for India and Pakistan. More generally, the clear focus of IDA on poorer countries and development, broadly defined, helped push the World Bank toward its own focus on global poverty, and an articulation of how it saw the broad remedies to it. Over time the criteria for judging performance as a central criterion for IDA allocation have become sharper and more elaborate (see Chapter 3).

The World Bank had operated with relative autonomy in its early years, in large measure because it did not depend on regular budget allocations from member governments and because borrowing countries repaid their loans on time and its financial borrowing program was so successful. The picture was quite different for IDA, which needed annual budget appropriations from governments in richer countries to continue significant levels of concessional lending. While IDA's replenishment rhythm took time to establish, it eventually fell into a pattern marked by regular successive multiyear negotiated agreements—most involving protracted discussions with donors, followed by further approval (authorization by the US Congress, especially) and then annual appropriations (see Table 2.1 which summarizes

Table 2.1 Successive replenishments of IDA resources and amounts

Replenishment label	IDA period (fiscal years)	Replenishment amounts[1] (million SDRs)
Initial (IDA0)	FY61–64	763
IDA1	FY65–68	924
IDA2	FY69–71	1,428
IDA3	FY72–74	2,738
IDA4	FY75–77	4,218
IDA5	FY78–80	6,193
IDA6	FY81–84	9,549
FY84 Account	FY84	1,318
Special Fund	FY84	519
IDA7	FY85–87	8,997
Special Facility for Africa	FY86–88	921
IDA8	FY88–90	11,677
IDA9	FY91–93	14,049
IDA10	FY94–96	16,274
Interim Trust Fund	FY97	2,228
IDA11	FY97–99	12,395
IDA12	FY00–02	15,312
IDA13	FY03–05	17,833
IDA14[2]	FY06–08	22,693
MDRI	FY07–44	22,737
IDA 15	FY09–11	TBD
Total		*172,765*

Source: "Compendium of IDA Financial Policies" (Washington DC: IDA, October 2006)

Notes:
[1] Includes donor contributions, internal resources, IBRD net income transfers and IFC designation from retained earnings.
[2] Includes donor resources to finance forgone charges on IDA13 grants.

IDA replenishments). IBRD began to grant some of its profits to IDA on a regular basis, but these funds represented only part of IDA's financial needs. As awareness of the extensive needs of poor countries grew, it also became apparent that the international economy and overall climate for aid would have a material impact on IDA and the rest of the World Bank Group. The days of the autonomous, low-key, and rather gray World Bank were coming to a close by the late 1960s.

The McNamara years

The year 1968 stands out as a watershed in World Bank history. President Lyndon B. Johnson nominated Robert S. McNamara as Bank president, and he immediately began to put his stamp on the institution. Indeed, many features of the Bank today have clear roots in the McNamara years.

Among them are the goal of raising and lending enough money to make a real dent in development needs, a focus on global poverty (what McNamara referred to as "the lowest 40 percent") as a central responsibility of the World Bank and its member governments, expansion into new arenas such as health, nutrition, and tourism, a strong focus on an elaborate process for programming projects, and the creation of an internal but independent mechanism for evaluating the Bank's own operations. Research to provide the intellectual foundation for development also assumed a far higher profile, and in turn brought the Bank itself far greater prominence. McNamara's speeches at the World Bank's annual meetings came to be markers of evolving development thinking, and the Bank's annual World Development Reports—each dedicated to a specific topic—became important catalysts for both theory and action. The result was that the World Bank underwent rapid staff growth and far-reaching reorganization, which emphasized the needs of the world's major regions and sought to link the economic and analytic work of the Bank with its highly developed project focus.[10]

Crisis upon crisis in a turbulent world

The first oil shock of 1973, in retrospect, marked the start of another major transformation for the World Bank. Underlying operations in the early years was an implicit assumption of a fairly orderly, linear progression toward greater prosperity—for individual countries and the world overall. Sound economic management and sound projects (the word "sound" was much used in the World Bank) were what was needed, with many common principles across countries. The oil shocks were followed by a lengthy period when many countries faced acute problems in servicing large private and public debt they had contracted. Both in turn led to and were often exacerbated by the deep-seated economic collapse threatening many countries, especially in Africa. These events all drove far-reaching overhauls that profoundly changed the World Bank.

The World Bank was either a central or a major player in crisis after economic crisis, expected to help finance looming gaps in external accounts to enable countries to meet their financial obligations and to continue to grow. These crises challenged the Bank's prior focus on project lending, because the need to finance national recovery and then a progressive "return" to development programs was obvious and urgent; and because—as became painfully and progressively apparent—projects simply could not succeed or even survive in a climate of economic crisis and policy mismanagement. In response, "structural adjustment" lending rapidly became a core focus in the growing number of affected countries, accompanied by a new emphasis on "conditionality." These developments gave economic advice and the analysis underlying it new bite and importance.

Structural adjustment lending entailed providing financial support to governments that agreed to macroeconomic reforms—reforms that were intended to transform their countries' basic economic structures in a fundamental way. Examples of structural adjustment measures included increases in energy prices, action to raise state revenues, and tariff reforms. Most such lending was agreed upon in a crisis setting, and the expectation was that the reforms would be sharp and short, allowing both a country and the World Bank to return to a "normal" development path. The focus was on "stroke-of-the-pen" reforms that could be quickly enacted. To ensure that a country would indeed undertake the reforms, and to clarify the Bank's role in providing funds (the financing had to be seen to achieve something), the reforms carried increasingly detailed requirements. As experience showed that countries often did not fulfill these promises, this "conditionality" became more and more specific, leading to hundreds of designated actions that, in retrospect, no one could possibly carry out or monitor. What's more, missing from most of these early structural reform efforts were consultations beyond a small set of financial officials, careful assessment of the impact of the reforms on societies and their political repercussions, and conscious efforts to inform and engage those affected.

In contrast to expectations, the new forms of lending were not short, sharp, and sweet (solving the problems even if painful), as initially expected. Rather, it became increasingly apparent that the roots of most crises were far deeper than initially understood, and could not be solved by stroke-of-the-pen macroeconomic reforms. The initial response from the Bank was to make the programs both broader and more specific, by extending them to major economic sectors and enterprises. Meanwhile, opposition to the painful reforms mounted, both within individual countries and globally.

The reform programs that the Bank recommended and supported did change to reflect experience and recognition of the depth of the problems. And much of the enduring negative image of structural adjustment programs—including the largely mythical view that the financial institutions actively required cuts in social spending—relates to a short period in the early years of adjustment lending. More recent programs built in elaborate consultation and information mechanisms, often require countries to make social spending a priority, and are linked to efforts to provide at least a partial safety net for those directly affected. The political economy of reform is also far better, if still imperfectly, understood.

The fundamental structural adjustment, however, occurred in analysts' understanding of the underlying problems and what needs to be done to fix them. Far from requiring short sharp seismic shifts in policy, the crises revealed the need for continuous reform extending to and linking all sectors of the economy. Such far-ranging reform requires an approach that is the polar opposite of secret programs negotiated by financiers in smoke-filled rooms. Though it is no longer or rarely called structural adjustment today, it is in fact central to the understanding of development today that a continuing commitment to reforms that are often far-reaching is essential to adapt to the rapidly changing economic environment that is part of the globalization revolution. The early blindness of many within the World Bank and even in governments concerned about the political and social dimensions of reforms has given way to better understanding. And the focus on a small battery of macroeconomic reforms, often quite divorced from project and sector experience, has changed to reflect particularly a focus on sectoral reforms and attention to governance, including the legal reforms, institutional facets of reform implementation, and concentration on budget processes, that alone can make sustained reform a reality.

The Bank's role in coordinating aid to many nations during these crises helped them to survive difficult times and also, in some instances, supported their far-ranging efforts at economic transformation (Bolivia, Colombia, Ghana, and the CFA franc zone in West Africa come to mind as examples). However, this period of crisis and focus on macroeconomic reforms also brought the World Bank into far more direct conflict with many development actors, especially with the IMF, parts of the UN system and in civil society, than ever before. This resulted in redefinitions of roles.

According to the architecture guiding the international financial institutions, the IMF is expected to take the lead in responding to economic and financial crises and providing macroeconomic advice. However, reality has proved much messier, and sparked tension between the two institutions. The Bank has usually not engaged in crises unless the IMF has been present, but some countries have sought direct Bank engagement without the Fund, and occasionally this has occurred. Leaders of the two institutions have hammered out formal agreements on their respective roles (worth special note is the IMF World Bank concordat of 1989 which defined respective responsibilities and areas of focus and several subsequent elaborations[11]), but practical realities and even personalities have determined how these roles actually play out—often country by country.

One product of the tensions between the Bank and the Fund, and uncoordinated or even contradictory advice from the Bretton Woods twins, was the Policy Framework Paper (PFP) mechanism, begun in 1986. Described by one early leader as an effort to "bang heads together," the PFP was to be a joint effort by a national government, the IMF, and the World Bank to create a framework and preconditions for "policy-based lending," approved separately by the boards of the IMF and World Bank.

The idea of creating a clearly articulated framework for reform was sound. The system did work well in some countries (Bolivia, and Uganda come to mind), and also gave the World Bank board a new mechanism for discussing country policy, which it had hitherto largely lacked. However, PFPs could be required only for IDA countries. And the process—often largely a fiction—of working out a common policy framework among three partners with very different mandates and styles proved cumbersome. International organizations and local leaders who were not part of the process regarded it as secretive. These problems led to an opening up of the process, and to some extent to its dilution. The PFP was in many respects the precursor to the Poverty Reduction Strategy Process (PRSP), which took shape early in the new century. (Chapter 3 delves more deeply into these reform efforts.)

The climax of this period of turbulence, crisis, and response was the East Asia crisis of 1997 to 1999. This economic crisis hit almost totally by surprise (some wise souls saw it coming, but for most actors it came out of the blue), and with a speed and contagion that again shocked thinking and practice. The financing needs and potential consequences of the crisis were without precedent in scale and urgency and the rapid contagion from one country to another and dramatic drops in production were shocking to all observers because they threatened not only major countries but the world's very financial system and architecture. All hands were mobilized to respond, with intense hour-by-hour involvement of the treasury departments of major countries (especially the United States), as well as the IMF, the World Bank, and the Asian Development Bank. The result was massive financial packages aimed above all at stabilizing country finances but also to support reforms that would support recovery, produced at record speed. Some $53 billion was mobilized for South Korea alone—with the World Bank's largest-ever financial operation, for $3 billion, negotiated and disbursed between Thanksgiving and Christmas of 1997, while the IMF approved a standby for Special Drawing Rights (SDR) 15.5 billion. It also sparked far ranging analysis and action to address what were seen as the roots of crisis, including the deeply flawed banking systems, widespread tolerance of corrupt practices, and neglect of social safety nets.

Much has been written about the management of the crisis, including the interplay between the IMF and the World Bank.[12] Several lessons stand out. The World Bank played a crucial role (in close contact with the IMF) in diagnosing and addressing the crisis in the financial sector, which was a fundamental part of the overall crisis, and one that left a lasting legacy, including new appreciation of the critical importance of sound financial systems. The Bank also made an extraordinary effort to address the social consequences of the crisis both in helping to fashion urgent measures to help people most directly affected and to rethink social policies in the wake of the profound changes that had taken place across most East Asian countries. The social focus came against a backdrop of weak social safety nets in East Asian countries and poor data on fast-moving events. The lesson that crisis response must include attention to social and political needs had been well learned. The crisis also put corruption squarely on the agenda, and the ensuing action and debates—especially but not solely regarding Indonesia where corruption and nepotism issues were at the heart of urgent demands for political reform—marked an important turning point.

The East Asia crisis appears to have made its mark in shedding light on how to handle economic emergencies; few since 1999 have exhibited the frightening speed and breadth of contagion across the world that sent shudders through all corners of global markets. Those events revealed that the economic crises of today are far more complex than their predecessors, as they move at a dizzying pace, with virtually no country immune to the contagion. The global mechanisms called upon to respond were ill-prepared and ill-equipped to meet the extraordinary needs, but respond they did, with an effort that has few parallels. Overall, the crisis demonstrated the potential for swift and coordinated response when crisis strikes, but also the need to develop more effective and broad-based global mechanisms for doing so.

The impact of geography on a global institution

Through all these tumultuous events, the World Bank has evolved from an institution serving a small group of countries in a still-colonial world, to a Cold War-shaped entity operating almost exclusively in the capitalist world, to a global organization with 185 members (with Cuba and North Korea among the few nonmembers; see Figure 2.1, and Maps 2.1 and 2.2).

The membership of the World Bank—along with that of IFC and MIGA—grew steadily during three major periods: during the 1960s, as previously colonized countries gained independence; in 1980, when the People's Republic of China decided to rejoin;[13] and after the fall of the Berlin Wall, the breakup of the former Soviet Union, and the

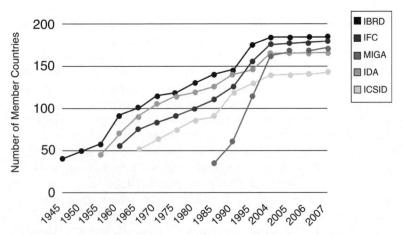

Figure 2.1 World Bank group: history of membership.
Source: World Bank Corporate Secretariat.

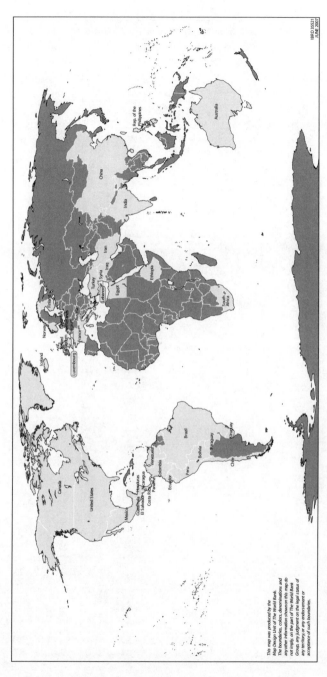

Map 2.1 World Bank member countries in 1948.

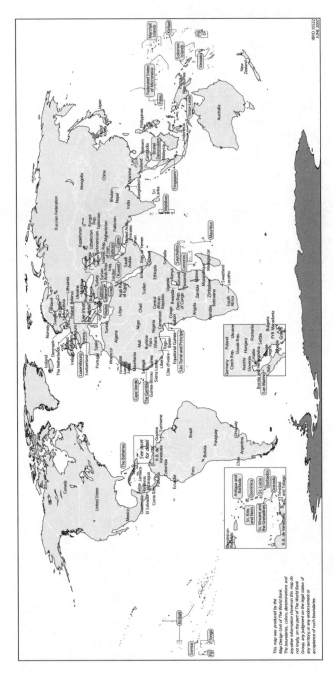

IBRD 35522
JUNE 2007

Map 2.2 World Bank member countries in 2007.

expansion of the Bank's operations to what came to be termed the "transition" countries.[14]

The changing geography of the Bank's membership has shaped its work and ethos. For example, the postcolonial transition that brought IDA into being, trained the Bank's attention far more sharply on Africa and, with time, on the deep and intractable problems of poverty. Bank leaders over the years underestimated the wide-ranging needs on that continent (48 countries in sub-Saharan Africa are now World Bank members), and the weakness of institutions that was an enduring legacy of colonialism. The Bank gradually expanded to meet the demands of this region, and today the African organizational complex within the Bank is the institution's largest by far. There is a broad recognition that the success or failure of global development efforts will in the future be shaped largely by how programs in Africa perform.

The Bank's global coverage presents important challenges, including the common question: what does it mean to be a "World Bank"? While the world's wealthier countries clearly still dominate the Bank's power structure, it has evolved into a pragmatic institution that operates within many economic and political systems. The journey from Bretton Woods to the World Bank of today has also taken it from unambiguous and largely unquestioned domination by the United States to a far more varied and challenging international perspective (though the weight of US influence remains a central governance issue for the institution). For example, when China decided to resume its World Bank membership in 1980, it set about the process with extraordinary diligence, studying Bank operations in other parts of the world and making clear that China would determine the nature of lending and other aspects of the relationship with the World Bank and other partners. The World Bank responded vigorously to the challenge and has managed the relationship with care and considerable skill, through times of success and far more difficult and controversial times including the Tiananmen Square events, the crisis over lending for the Western China poverty project (which provoked anger from supporters of Tibet), and current unease over China's growing role in Africa. The Bank's intellectual work, in particular, has garnered considerable admiration, even as its relationships with China have drawn criticism— notably for joint unwillingness to address directly human rights issues.

China was the Bank's largest and one of its most successful borrowers for many years, peaking at $2 billion annually. Indeed, China almost hit the ceiling the Bank imposed on the share of its portfolio that single country could hold (12 percent), requiring an elaborate agreement to allow operations to continue. The Chinese government was clearly the driving force behind this relationship, but it relied on excellent analytic work by the Bank, and well-prepared lending has yielded excellent results. The China operation stands apart in many respects, but the experience has had repercussions far beyond in setting both a model of country leadership and in showing what a country can accomplish in poverty reduction in a remarkably short time.

The end of the Cold War in 1989 sparked a transition that was also a transformational event for the World Bank. With several notable exceptions (Yugoslavia, Poland, and Czechoslovakia, at different times), the World Bank had been entirely absent from the communist world. Suddenly, with the thaw in Eastern Europe, and then the collapse and breakup of the Soviet Union, a group of new countries with distinctive demands joined the Bank. It pursued wide-ranging operations in those countries almost from the start, putting particular emphasis on supporting the privatization of state-owned enterprise and developing a wide range of institutions, especially the missing market-focused institutions that could support new private sector roles, but also reforms in sectors like health, education, and environment. The Bank has been particularly active in the former Yugoslavia, and has worked closely with the European Bank for Reconstruction and Development in the region.

A new phase has come with the "graduation" of several Eastern European countries from Bank lending, and the entry of several into the European community. The Bank is clearly phasing out its direct lending role in those countries.

Opening to civil society and "50 Years Is Enough"

The McNamara years marked a high point for the World Bank, though it was not always obvious at the time. His successors, A.W. Claussen, Barber Conable, and Lewis Preston, presided over more complicated eras. The rather heady and complacent World Bank began to encounter increasing opposition, which included, perhaps most significantly, pressing calls to open its closely held information to civil society and media. Pressed initially by environmental activists but increasingly encouraged by broader civil society groups and by advocates from inside the World Bank, a gradual process, with fits and starts and some reluctance, pried open many parts of the Bank. First a single civil society representative, then a unit, reflected this process of transformation from secretive, government-focused institution to an organization more ready to engage in an era of globalization and public accountability. But these early openings were often too little and too late for the tides sweeping the world.

By the time the Bank's fiftieth anniversary (in 1994) began to approach, Bank leaders and supporters were aware that the institution was facing a crisis of significant proportions. The crisis had two major manifestations: serious doubts expressed by the executive directors, and thus member governments who held the purse strings about the Bank's budget proposals; and mounting protests directed at the Bank by civil society critics. The leading edge of the protests involved environmental concerns—especially the World Bank's support for large dam projects—but these criticisms expanded to cover other areas, including structural adjustment, and in some cases represented jugular protests against the Bank's entire approach and its very existence. The 50 Years Is Enough campaign was clear in its message. (Chapter 6 will delve more deeply into these critiques.)

After a period of something akin to a bunker mentality, wherein Bank leaders trusted that the protests would simply fade, the Bank responded more forthrightly and embarked on major internal reform. As a leader of a task force put it, the Bank faced a choice between failure to change, leading to obsolescence and death, and a major revamping that could make it the world's premier development institution. The path to reform was seen as including a greater focus on the needs of individual countries, a major effort to enhance staff skills through recruitment and training, and a lightening of the bureaucratic burdens, that were seen as making the Bank cumbersome and unresponsive and expensive to do business with.

"Client focus" thus became the watchword of the day, with the goal of giving the Bank more of what was regarded as the best of the private sector—a nimbleness demanding excellence, and competition injected into the way staff were assigned and their employment contracts. What emerged was a "matrix structure" designed to build strong centers of technical excellence but allow teams to form in response to specific needs. Much of the thinking behind this reform process continues to shape the Bank today, even after several reorganization projects, notably in 1997.

The Wolfensohn Bank

James D. Wolfensohn became president of the World Bank in June 1995, while this campaign by critics was still unfolding. He arrived with unprecedented enthusiasm for the job: he may have been the only president who actively sought the position over many years after a varied career, and his extraordinary personal skills in many domains—finance, culture, sports—won him the enduring title of "renaissance president."

His entry was rather stormy, as he heard countless criticisms of the Bank, not least from the staff itself, and, with an energy level that few can parallel, set out to make his mark on the institution.[15]

He first focused on Africa, but also he set out to travel the world, visiting over 120 countries during his ten years as president. He was fearless in voicing what he did not like, but also passionate in his enthusiasm. Six of the many initiatives that he launched or encouraged illustrate the scope of his ideas and influence.

The first two were breaking the taboo that made it difficult to discuss corruption openly at the Bank, and putting HIV/AIDS far more boldly on the development agenda. At a major speech in Hong Kong, Wolfensohn spoke out about the "cancer of corruption," and he often noted that he was told not to mention the "c" word because it crossed the line into politics and thus was off the Bank's turf. But Wolfensohn made a strong case that corruption was destructive to development in many ways, and that it therefore belonged on the Bank's agenda. He also boldly committed the Bank to playing a central role in fighting the HIV/AIDS pandemic, assuring that funding would never be the binding constraint (a promise, of course, that has yet to be fulfilled at a global level). The scope of the World Bank's HIV/AIDS programs, which had inched forward against resistance from many country leaders as well as Bank staff, increased dramatically though they only began to meet the enormous needs of people living with and dying of AIDS, especially in Africa.

Wolfensohn was struck by the institution's seemingly narrow focus on economic analysis, and responded with what came to be known as the "comprehensive development framework," or CDF. The core message was that the economic and social aspects of development were like "breathing out and breathing in," and he insisted on recognizing the complexities of the development process, and thus of the Bank's work. He reflected that complexity by constantly reaching out to groups previously remarkably neglected by the Bank, notably youth, cultural leaders, the disabled, and faith leaders and communities, as well as communities like the Roma (traditionally called Gypsies). He was also deeply moved by what he saw of poverty, and often echoed the influential Voices of the Poor work, the pioneering Bank effort to survey poor communities and people across the world and portray poverty in their own words.[16]

In all these cases he launched specific projects and programs to make the commitments more tangible. He also pursued creative partnerships across many sectors, including the private sector, foundations, civil society organizations, other multilateral banks, and the artistic community. The backlash against CDF was sharp at times, and the numerous ideas he launched posed demanding questions about the Bank's role, and whether it had the resources and the mandate to undertake the new work. Nonetheless, these initiatives wove their way into the World Bank's ethos (though economic thought continues to be rather dominant and some of the initiatives he cherished were endangered following his departure).

Wolfensohn also focused considerable attention on the role of women, in both the Bank itself and the development process (with considerable encouragement from his wife, Elaine Wolfensohn). Until the early 1970s, the Bank had been almost entirely male-dominated (the official history of the first 25 years barely mentions women). However, starting with the encouragement if not the passionate support of Robert McNamara, and the full engagement of Barber Conable, the Bank began to address the important roles that women play in development, and the linked subject of women as professional staff of the Bank itself. Progress on both fronts was rather slow, but early women leaders were determined and effective in advancing their cause, and sterling work on issues such as the education of girls gradually helped establish both the importance and legitimacy of focusing more sharply on women. Wolfensohn continued to support these efforts through his early and strong advocacy of the UN's Beijing Women's Summit in 1995.

Another Wolfensohn cause was training, reflected in his insistence that all managers go through a solid financial training program (so they could "read a balance sheet"), and in his strong support for expanding the World Bank Institute, the Bank's knowledge and capacity development arm. He also focused, particularly in his final years, on capacity building as essential to a comprehensive approach to development.

A final area that deserves mention is Wolfensohn's continued attention to what he termed the "knowledge bank." This reflected his fascination with the ways that information technology was transforming life and business, including development, and he pressed the Bank staff hard to be at the forefront of the information revolution, not dragging behind on the caboose. Toward this end he launched the ambitious Development Gateway, designed to bring together in a giant web site and database information on development ideas and projects. He also pressed hard to launch a Global Distance Learning Network, which uses state-of-the-art videoconferencing to provide flexible training courses and conferences.

Wolfensohn's wide-ranging concerns positioned the Bank to move into or expand work in other arenas as well, including a return to its original mandate on reconstruction, and greater focus on the environment (including global warming). He also pressed the institution to focus more actively on poor communities, especially by bringing his personal energy, passion and determination to the Bank's stated goal of working to end poverty. He gave the institution extraordinarily high visibility, serving as a voice consistently advocating for poor people and communities, and he himself traveled widely and reached out to a vast array of groups, especially in civil society and business. This invited admiration but also concerns that the reach of the World Bank was exceeding its grasp and its capacity.

Reconstruction after natural disasters and war

Although the Bank largely took a backseat in postwar reconstruction after the launch of the Marshall Plan, it has frequently been at the fore of major rebuilding efforts after natural disasters such as earthquakes, hurricanes, and postwar conflicts. Indeed, the Bank has often shown its best side in mobilizing expertise and resources with unexpected flair and rapidity, and has developed considerable skill in responding to such disasters. The major role that the World Bank played after the Asian tsunami of December 2004 is a notable example, as it quickly pulled together programs—$835 million as of June 2005—to the countries affected by the tsunami, including management of a large ($500 million) multi-donor trust fund to bring together the mammoth reconstruction efforts. The Bank has also played an important role in rebuilding after armed conflicts. Notable examples include the Bank's active efforts immediately following the independence of Bangladesh, and post-conflict work in the Democratic Republic of the Congo, the Balkans, East Timor, and Liberia and Sierra Leone.

The complexities of post-conflict reconstruction gave rise to much reflection in the late 1990s, which in turn produced a still-unfinished agenda for the Bank. The expected path of rebuilding—with neat phases separating conflict, peace negotiations, reconstruction, and resumption of development—often did not conform with reality, and UN organizations (notably the High Commissioner for Refugees) pressed for a more comprehensive and sophisticated approach. They were especially eager to assure earlier World Bank funding of the transitional phases that would ideally link peacemaking, post-conflict work, and then development. It also became clear, given recurring conflicts in many countries, that it made little sense to rebuild if those efforts did not address the causes of conflict. The World Bank began to engage more actively in analysis and action involving conflict situations.

Moreover, the global community too often found itself trapped in a situation where a nation's legacy of unpaid debts blocked funding for reconstruction; international plans to forgive such debt were always in the offing, but they took time and effort, delaying essential work on the ground. These experiences (and the respected work of Paul Collier, a professor of economics at Oxford who spent several years at the Bank) led to the creation of a special Post-Conflict Fund, and growing recognition that the institution would almost always be a major player after armed conflict.

Fallout and creation: environmental impact

The World Bank came rather slowly to seeing itself as a prominent player in the environmental protection and global environmental debate. The Bank's response in this arena was heavily shaped by protests against specific projects, especially India's mammoth Narmada Dam, and the Bank's active promotion of development affecting the Amazon region of Brazil.[17] Early environmental work tended to be rather partial and defensive. The Bank's role in some cases was defined by what it did not do (for example in declining to support the Three Gorges Dam project in China which went ahead with other financing).

However, Bank leaders were eventually convinced that environmental critiques had merit, and the overall attitude about such issues began to shift (the children of leaders may have been an important force in encouraging such change). Younger staff members were deeply committed to environmental protection, and the environmental staff expanded from a tiny core to a large and prominent team with broad expertise. Critical minimum environmental standards also became part of fundamental operating policies, which ensured full environmental as well as social assessments of projects, and protection of cultural property. The Bank staff working on environment steadily expanded. Today a central concern is whether these standards may be so high, and the weight of fulfilling them so burdensome, that countries shy away from asking the Bank for support.

Environmental debates were the drivers behind two important new components of the Bank: the Global Environmental Facility (GEF), and the Inspection Panel. Both are described in the next chapters as they function today. The GEF is a fund created in 1991 and housed at the Bank that provides direct support for environmental projects. The Inspection Panel, created in 1996, allows individuals and groups to file appeals seeking appropriate remedies if Bank-financed projects produce harmful effects because they fail to follow policy guidelines.

Tackling poverty and debt

From the days of Robert McNamara, the World Bank has seen itself as a global leader in combating poverty and bringing material benefits to the world's poorest communities. McNamara's questions about whether projects focused on the "lowest 40 percent" inspired the development of elaborate systems for analyzing poverty at the country level, and various global reporting mechanisms. A tradition that the World Development Report would address poverty at the turn of each decade led to major analyses in 1990 and 2000 and follow-up work. Two phrases proposed by a cohort of Bank managers as a vision statement—"Our dream is a world free of poverty," and "Fighting poverty with passion and professionalism"—resonated so strongly that when the institution inaugurated new headquarters in 1996, the first phrase was prominent at the front door. Today the commitment of the staff to the Bank's antipoverty mission is almost part of the water.

However, two vital questions remain. First, what does "poverty" mean? And second, what is the best way to fight it? These questions lie at the heart of much debate both within and about the Bank.

Put rather crudely, the debates suggest two understandings of poverty— one focused on income, the other more subtle, refined, and complex, taking into account the concept's social, psychological, material, and political dimensions. The Bank's heavy reliance on per capita income to categorize countries, and its use of $1 or $2 dollar a day as its most widely cited benchmark, fuels the view that income is its main criterion for assessing poverty. The Human Development Index, created by the UNDP, aims in part to counter this oversimplification.

However, in practice, the World Bank has never relied exclusively on a single or crude income measure of poverty, and certainly does not today, and it recognizes the oversimplification of the $1- or $2-dollar-a-day measure. The Voices of the Poor effort, varied poverty assessments, analysis and programs that address social capital and social exclusion, and countless other dimensions of the Bank's work reveal its complex understanding of poverty, which has only deepened over the years.

An important core issue turning around the role of economic growth in combating poverty has sparked intense debates, particularly around the World Development Report 2000, which focused on poverty. The draft of the report, which occasioned the debate, took the view that growth was essential for fighting poverty, *but* that in addition it was essential to look to two additional factors—investing in human capital through education and health, and assuring that safety nets were able to protect those groups that did not benefit from economic growth. The debates made clear that there were indeed different ways to see the issues and they often led to different remedies, policies and programs. The "growth-is-primary" school tends to focus on macro-economic policies to fight poverty, especially to encourage private investment, thus creating jobs and generating revenue to fund social services. This view can be characterized as "all boats will rise with the tide." More subtle versions of this argument stress that jobs cannot be created and funds for education and health will be insufficient without economic growth. Competing arguments hold that balanced, "pro-poor" growth cannot succeed without investments in human capital, or growth will always leave some behind. Affirmative policies must address the needs of excluded groups (women, disadvantaged youth, ethnic minorities), and efforts to build a social safety net must precede or at least accompany growth-based economic policies. This oversimplified picture reflects a healthy, essential and continuing debate within the Bank, turning on the complex dimensions of the World Bank's mandate, and its multifaceted work and staff.

These long-standing debates about the causes and remedies of poverty, with their repercussions for debates about aid focus and effectiveness, have come rather slowly to terms with the fundamental change in the global landscape that results from immense increases in private-sector financial flows. Whereas official development assistance was the main source of funds for most developing countries three decades ago, today private-sector investment dwarfs such assistance, especially in the fastest growing regions.

Equity: the theme of the future

Although the World Bank does not address security issues directly, at least two major developments arose at least in part from the events of 11 September 2001, and built on the active ensuing debates.

The first has been more incisive examination of "global balance"— the impact of inequality on relationships among nations, and on the fight against poverty. The imbalance between rich and poor nations is nothing new. What has changed is that contemporary international tensions highlight the mounting anger against rich nations and richer segments within them as well as in developing country societies. The combination of instant and vivid communication of this reality and the growing role of nonstate actors prompted James Wolfensohn to speak out repeatedly about the "world without walls," and the unfairness and dangers of the obvious global imbalance.

Although the Universal Declaration of Human Rights and many other modern documents reflect issues of social justice and equity, 9/11 forcibly inserted them more directly into discussions of global poverty. The World Development Report 2006, which focused on equity and development, highlighted the importance of ensuring a level playing field, for a start by providing universal access to education and healthcare, and by opening opportunities once closed by regulation or discrimination. A word came to be heard with greater urgency: unfairness, as the magnitude of global imbalance was increasingly difficult to ignore and called, with increasing urgency, for action to assure greater equity.

The second important repercussion of the 9/11 watershed is growing concern about the link between poverty and insecurity. Poverty and terrorism are obviously related only indirectly—the vast majority of poor people do not become terrorists, and most terrorists are far from poor. However, it is also very clear that where poverty persists and people lack hope for a better future, anger grows. The seemingly hopeless situation of countries and societies left behind is both a travesty of justice and fairness and a dangerous source of insecurity with global repercussions.

The World Bank has devoted much discussion to the difficult question of how it can and should approach 29 nations grouped under the infelicitous label of Low Income Countries under Stress (LICUS), or, more recently, fragile states, a group with a combined population of about 500 million. This question is knotty because experience makes it abundantly clear that investments in weak states are unsuccessful under most circumstances, and because by their nature these countries are not easy to work in. A task force recommended that the World Bank take an active and creative role in fostering change in these countries notably by supporting capacity building and efforts to define clear and positive development paths and by continuing support for basic human needs programs. This would help meet real needs of poor people and allow the World Bank to be ready to respond when windows of opportunity open. More broadly, the focus on human security, reflected in UN debates and in the approach of widely ranging organizations including the Religions for Peace (WCRP), which organized its August 2006 global assembly around the concept of "shared security," illustrates a blending of the traditionally very separate worlds of security and development.[18]

The Wolfowitz era

The short presidency of Paul Wolfowitz (June 2005–June 2007) will be remembered above all for the extraordinary and protracted controversy that brought it to its premature close. Wolfowitz came to the Bank with a difficult legacy, because of his prominent role in launching and prosecuting the war in Iraq that began in 2003. He faced three special challenges as a result. He needed first to demonstrate that he had made the shift from a US official to an international civil servant, by changes in style, approach, and stance setting himself apart from the policies of the US administration. Second, he needed to find ways to build both trust and understanding within a notoriously difficult international bureaucracy, establishing alliances and finding ways to understand the institution. And third, he needed to establish at least the first indications of his strategic approach to leading development issues. He failed on all three counts, opening himself through both personnel appointments and actions to the perception that he remained closely tied to US objectives, people and policies. He attempted to run the Bank through aides who he brought with him and alienated many respected Bank leaders. His two "strategic initiatives," to focus on Africa and to fight corruption more aggressively, were, in the first instance seen as obvious and hardly a new departure and in the second as clumsy and arbitrary because his actions to fight corruption were pursued without sufficient consultation and engagement of the World Bank staff or, indeed, its Board and shareholders.

But the final, large straw was a controversy surrounding his handling of his partner, Shaha Riza, an eight-year Bank employee, which opened him to accusations of dual standards and hypocrisy (see Figure 2.2). After several months of exchanges which illustrated how far the Bank had become an open institution (so much material came out that the notion of leaks lost their meaning) and a media blitz, Wolfowitz reluctantly resigned. Despite wide calls for an open selection process internationally, the old tradition of looking to the US to name the Bank's president prevailed (probably because of a deal struck as part of Wolfowitz's resignation and fueled by European hopes of keeping their right to name the IMF Managing Director). Following President Bush's nomination of Robert Zoellick, former US Trade Representative and Deputy Secretary of State, the board confirmed his appointment as President with effect from 1 July 2007.

Summary

The World Bank has undergone a profound metamorphosis over its history. It began as an institution created primarily to finance the immense reconstruction needs after World War II, grew as an institution largely serving the capitalist world during the Cold War era, and

Figure 2.2 The Wolfowitz controversy illustrated.

has become (albeit with considerable challenge and controversy) a truly global player, the world's leading development institution and a major voice and actor in economic and social development and the quest for equity of poorer nations. The contemporary World Bank is deeply engaged in all three challenges: reconstruction, development, and equity.

The World Bank's history reflects tumultuous historical developments. Theories about economic and social change have shifted the ground radically during its lifetime and shaped its course even as the Bank has itself shaped the understanding of what development entails. Themes woven through the Bank's history are the roles of its president and board, the tensions between a country and a global focus, raising funds for its operations, and how the Bank, whose articles prohibit political involvement, navigates the obviously political shoals that are part of social and economic change and thus development. The changing geography of the Bank's membership has shaped the World Bank's work and ethos, as it has expanded in size to be virtually a global institution. Major markers were the arrival of newly independent African nations, the rejoining of China in 1980, and the period when the former Soviet Union and Eastern European nations joined the World Bank. Successive presidents have left important marks, especially Robert McNamara and James Wolfensohn and (in a negative sense) Paul Wolfowitz.

3   Nuts and bolts
How the World Bank functions

The World Bank is not a simple study, and understanding how it functions is far from easy. The World Bank operates in an extraordinary variety of countries and situations, and programs it supports are continuously adapting to widely different realities as well as changing world circumstances and agendas. A vast body of historical experience and accumulated case history guides the World Bank's actions and practices; indeed, a deliberate reliance on precedents and the desire to ensure fairness across countries often dampens appetite and will for bold new initiatives. As a public institution with countless stakeholders, formal and informal, holding it constantly to account, the World Bank is subject to multiple layers of complexity which often translate into heavy bureaucracy and slow decision-making. Beyond excellent reasons for varied and nuanced approaches, a tendency to complexity also seems part of the institution's DNA, derived both from governance arrangements and the culture of sophisticated analysis engrained in staff practice and the academic disciplines in which they are trained. Successive efforts to simplify Bank policies and procedures have had a Sisyphean quality, with an ever-growing battery of new units, policies, and practices emerging despite sincere and intensive efforts to streamline. The image of a supertanker or large giant pervades many observations of the World Bank, reflecting both its size relative to other development institutions and the common perception and experience of slow change or even inertia.

An important if seemingly contradictory and counterintuitive reality (set against this backdrop of complexity and cumbersome procedures), is that the World Bank often does operate with creativity and impact and sometimes great speed. The best results are achieved and the bureaucratic shoals well navigated when three circumstances are present (and especially if they come together): a propelling crisis (like the tsunami or the East Asian financial crisis), strong pressures from a key member government (as during the West African CFA franc devaluation) or the Bank's own leaders (as for HIV/AIDS when Wolfensohn pressed for a large multicountry response), and skillful appreciation by those concerned of the background and intent of policies and procedures combined with persistence and determination to move ahead (community development in Indonesia and early social funds are examples). More broadly, there is actually far more leeway and innovation involving the Bank at field levels than is often appreciated (even by Bank staff).

These facts of World Bank life (the bad, the ugly and the good) must be recognized to appreciate how the Bank works and why, and because almost any description of a Bank function, policy, or practice can be countered with an exceptional circumstance. This chapter provides a map to help people navigate the territory, with signposts focused on the reasons for different policies and practices, and suggestions on where to find answers to questions.[1]

The chapter offers an account of standard World Bank practice at the country level; the Bank's substantive work in different technical sectors; its intellectual work—that is, its research and analysis; its organizational structure and challenges; its staff; and its funding: where the money comes from, and how it is managed. The chapter also explores the question of how the Bank judges its effectiveness and results, and outlines the recourse people outside the Bank may have in case of complaints. Finally it presents some overall facts and figures that give an indication of size and scope. It can be read juxtaposed with Chapter 5 which provides more examples of policies in operation on the ground.

To help in setting the scene and appreciating the goals and ideal standards against which operations are designed, the chapter starts with a brief portrayal of an idealized—and thus fictional—way that the World Bank might operate in an individual country, contrasted with a less ideal, also fictional account of how the World Bank and the development community may appear from different vantage points.

A tale of the World Bank ideal

Utania,[2] a small territory on the continent of Lector, finally won agreement from Enfandia, its colonial ruler, that it would become independent two years hence, giving it lead time to prepare for elections and build key state institutions and policies. Utania faced numerous challenges—not least its legacy of a long period of instability and armed conflict, the poverty of most of its people, rampant disease, flawed education and health networks that reached only a fraction of the people, weak banks, a reputation for corruption and misgovernance that left business and the public mistrustful, and a litany of worries about long-standing illegal forest cutting, sex trafficking, and child labor. Despite these challenges, Utania abounded with natural resources, and its coming independence sparked excitement and hope.

The United Nations (UN) was centrally involved in negotiating Utania's independence and peace, working in harmony with Enfandia, now Utania's supporter and mentor in global discussions. A UN special representative organized talks between Utania and Enfandia, which were led by Utania's political organizations and included people from previously excluded groups (the meetings were composed of 50 percent women, for example). Thoughtful discussions resulted in solid agreement on the strategic priorities proposed by Utanians (including education, health, critical infrastructure, banking reforms, smallholder agriculture, and microcredit initiatives), and in a skillfully defined plan for support from other countries and organizations based on their experience and comparative advantage. It was at this stage that the World Bank became informally involved (behind the scenes) in the discussions and background work to support proposals.

The United Nations Development Programme (UNDP) agreed to coordinate external partners, the International Monetary Fund (IMF) was to support macroeconomic and financial programs, the United Nations Children's Fund (UNICEF) would lead support from external entities (including various international civil society organizations) for youth and children, and Enfandia agreed to support massive training and capacity-building programs, because it shared language and cultural affinities with Utania. A major private foundation agreed to fund a neutral review of Utania's natural resources and environmental options. Participants in these efforts agreed to clear performance objectives, benchmarks, and measurement of results. These efforts would, for the aid community overall, be perfectly calibrated with the Millennium Development Goals, which would serve as an overall guide and provided specific targets.

The World Bank was to play three major roles in the transition period. First, it would define Utania's need for development financing and help mobilize and coordinate it, in the process working to create systems for public investment. Second, the Bank would support the intellectual underpinning for Utania's development by spearheading collaborative studies in priority sectors. These studies would provide sound guidelines for safeguarding Utania's environmental, social, and cultural heritage, propose priorities for fighting poverty, and assess the climate for private-sector investment. Third, the Bank would support planning and implementation of a community development program, sectoral programs for health and education, key infrastructure investments, and an annual financing review to ensure that the fledgling government would have sufficient and predictable resources.

The plans were implemented smoothly, with the UN leading monitoring of an exemplary national election, followed by well-prepared local and municipal elections. Efforts to build Utania's capacity were so successful that the handover of government functions from Enfandia to the new nation went off without a hitch, as trained Utanians assumed their new posts. Teams of external advisors adhered to a carefully planned schedule that fully coordinated their work and ensured that they communicated their findings clearly and transparently to the government and each other, and posted them on an active new web site. Monthly video conferences allowed development partners (bilaterals and other MBDs) to provide full action reports.

The World Bank convened an annual financing meeting in Utania's capital attended by all partners, including representatives of civil society and faith leaders. The meetings focused on strategy and cutting edge innovations, bringing in leading entrepreneurs and thinkers to look to the path ahead. Participants also dealt with a few bothersome instances of improper use of funds swiftly and effectively, reported on progress on each step in the development plan, and made mid-course corrections. Government decision-makers deeply appreciated professional, objective advice on how to address emerging issues—notably relations with local companies and two major multinational firms interested in investing in the promising new country.

Over 20 years, Utania was transformed from a troubled, very poor territory with uncertain prospects to a thriving nation known for its exemplary management of resources, its intense focus on human development, and the sensitivity and wisdom of its approaches to both national and global challenges. The involvement of various development partners changed steadily as they moved away from the direct engagement and strategic and coordinating roles of the pre- and post-independence years toward more specific technical advice. The World Bank helped to construct a much smaller and more targeted development financing scheme for Utania; it was heartening that the full community including the World Bank could mark the twentieth anniversary of their partnership with the recognition that the nation would soon be able to fund most of its development needs from its own resources and private investment. Under a new agreement, the Bank would provide technical assistance in sophisticated areas such as public debt management and sovereign wealth management, partially paid for by Utania, while the country would itself provide development advice to several poor countries in the region.

More complex realities and differing perspectives

The Utanian ideal is obviously a harmonious fiction, but it highlights several critical dimensions of how the World Bank aspires to operate:

- As a member of a well-orchestrated development partnership.
- With the lead squarely fixed with an individual country—primarily from its public sector, but also engaging its private sector and civil society.
- Through a careful combination of intellectual, catalytic, technical, and financial support.
- Through "best of the art" creative leadership in identifying economic and social priorities and options.
- Based on continuous and demanding evaluation of performance and learning from experience, those lessons well reflected in programs.
- Under a steady evolution from heavier engagement when countries face severe poverty problems and have weak capacity to a more hands-off relationship as circumstances permit.

Ideally such a path leads a country to "graduate" from direct Bank lending, with the nation's role gradually shifting from receiver to provider of advice. Examples of "graduates" include Ireland, Greece, and the Czech Republic.

At its best, the World Bank achieves most of these goals—though probably never in a single situation. In practice, development partnerships are generally messy and poorly coordinated, with too much competition and too little real harmony and genuine cooperation (see Chapter 4). The Bank clearly understands the need for nations to "own" and lead their development, and this is an oft-stated priority. However, pressures from donors and development fads constantly challenge this resolve, and there are too many cases where programs are poorly adapted to the realities of individual countries. The World Bank does focus continually on the different facets and phases of its ideal involvement, but articulation among them is often weak, with the result, for example, that the Bank's macroeconomic analysis often does not reflect its experience with actual projects, and vice versa.

The ideal course from poverty to success and prosperity almost always comes with detours, bumps on the road, disappointments, and fresh starts. Excellence is the objective, but it is often in the eye of the beholder, and sustaining a high standard across all aspects of World Bank involvement is far easier in theory than in practice. "More of the same" is too often the norm as bold departures are difficult to achieve. Evaluation and monitoring are part of the tool kit but are not always fully integrated into plans, with the result that piles of thick reports often gather dust.

It is worth recalling that tensions and differing views are not only healthy but essential in any endeavor—but especially in the development business, where uncertainties prevail, and each issue presents onion layers of complexity and difficult ethical as well as practical choices. Development practitioners recognize that there is simply no "magic bullet," no single path to successful development.

A further important and healthy reality is that different actors will view situations very differently. A macroeconomist is likely to focus on a positive investment climate and fiscal policy as development priorities; one economist from the IMF asserted during a strategic discussion of a country in crisis, "What's wrong with zero inflation as priority number one?" An education specialist is more likely to view education reform and expanding girls' access to schooling as leading priorities, while an environmentalist will focus on measures to halt forest cutting and the transport specialist on the compelling call to invest in port and road infrastructure. Debates about actions, options, and motivations can be laced through with both hope and anger and frequent poor communications are often part of the picture. The contrasting perspectives that emerge about a country (even a small one, like the Gambia) can seem to create a cacophony of difference, but taking the varying perspectives into account is both the essence of the development process and the central mission of the ideal World Bank.[3] These contrasting pictures (the Utanian ideal and the reality of disconnects and divergent perspectives) are, please recall, hypothetical, and are designed first to reflect how World Bank leaders might hope that the contemporary development process unfolds, and second to acknowledge the reality that performance often falls short of the ideal.

Operations within individual countries

Relationships with individual countries are the heart of World Bank operations. There is no mold; there are as many different relationships as there are countries, and those relationships take on different features over time. Amid the maze of operational challenges, history, and practices in individual nations, five features have special importance: the Bank's classification of a country into one of several categories; the process for creating a development strategy for that country; operational work in the country, including both advice and lending; the "country team"; and efforts to assess performance and adapt the course along the way.

The Utanian example of a country's ideal path from prostrate poverty to sustained performance and prosperity highlights an important feature of the World Bank's engagement: its long-term nature. The Bank is a partner for the long haul. The Utanian tale also illustrates the fact that relationships between the Bank and individual countries change over time, significantly. The evolution of the relationship with China (noted in Chapter 2) is a prime example but so are the very different phases of relationships with countries like Vietnam, Bolivia, the Ivory Coast, Venezuela, Mexico, and Albania.

Members of the World Bank fall into five broad groups (plus special cases), depending on their capacity to manage development assistance, ability to mobilize the resources they need, and development momentum. While there is some overlap and important common elements, the different country groupings have broad operational implications, beyond lending terms:

- *Creditworthy borrowers from the International Bank for Reconstruction and Development (IBRD), often termed middle-income countries.* Per capita incomes in this group (Mexico, Brazil, and Thailand, for example) are below the IBRD graduation threshold (see below) but too high for the countries to be eligible for "credits" (loans on highly concessional terms) or grants from the International Development Association (IDA) (the ceiling for IDA lending is revised each year and was $1,025 in 2007). Some of these countries elect not to borrow from IBRD, but the Bank often provides analysis and advice (South Africa, Gulf States).
- *Countries that borrow only from IDA, not from the IBRD.* Per capita income levels in these nations make them eligible for IDA credits, but they are not considered creditworthy for IBRD loans. Almost all African countries fall into this category. IDA strategies and instruments as well as the fate of replenishment discussions have critical importance for these countries.
- *IDA/IBRD "blend" countries.* These countries are eligible for both IDA (by per capita income) and IBRD lending (by creditworthiness standards), and elect to borrow from both.[4] India and Nigeria are examples.
- *Member countries that are not eligible for either IBRD or IDA lending because of armed conflict, economic mismanagement, or*

failure to service World Bank debts. These countries included (in mid-2007) Sudan and Myanmar/Burma. The World Bank maintains a fairly low level of operational work in most such countries, sometimes termed a "watching brief."

• *Special cases, especially countries in post-conflict and post-crisis situations.* Some countries that are ineligible for IDA or IBRD financing nonetheless participate in a multi-donor program financed by special funds, often administered in trust by the World Bank. Liberia in early 2007 presented such a case, as did Timor Leste immediately prior to its independence, the Occupied Palestinian Territories, and Iraq.

• *Countries considered too rich to borrow from the World Bank.* The World Bank today operates only in countries that fall below certain per capita income thresholds and the ideal is that countries progressively "graduate" from the need for Bank lending. The Bank periodically adjusts a per capita income ceiling that determines eligibility to borrow; in mid-2007, few countries with per capita incomes above $6,000 were IBRD borrowers. When a country reaches this level, discussions on a strategy for graduation begin. Prominent graduates include Ireland, Greece, Czechoslovakia, Singapore, and South Korea. As an aside, the World Bank has twice considered and agreed to a "de-graduation"—wherein countries that had ended their lending relationship ran into difficulties and sought renewed World Bank support (Venezuela in 1989 and South Korea in 1997).

These broad groupings do not translate into rigid operational practice (except insofar as they dictate lending terms, which are quite strictly determined by rules). They do, however, provide a general indication of the likely nature and level of World Bank work in a given country. Further, the category into which a country falls has complex but real implications for Bank budget allocations; in general, poorer countries are supposed to merit higher allocations of staff time on each task, to reflect greater "embedded" technical assistance. Suffice it to say that budget battles are waged constantly and the logic of allocations is rarely obvious, but the idea is that resources should follow needs and proven performance.

The first place to look in exploring World Bank work on and in a given country is the Country Assistance Strategy (CAS)—sometimes described as the Bank's "business plan." The CAS is a central vehicle for planning work in a given country, assessing how the Bank judges that country's prospects and development strategies, exploring and refining relationships among development partners, and summarizing the common agenda. Today the CAS emerges from a complex process that includes Bank discussions with government officials, public consultation, and internal discussions (especially about lending levels, benchmarks for judging performance and thus shifting among different scenarios, and budget implications). The Bank's executive directors formally consider, often with in-depth discussion, each CAS, and in virtually all cases it becomes a public document in its final incarnations. An innovation applied in a few countries—and probably a harbinger for the future, is a Joint Assistance Strategy—which involves several development partners in a similar process (Uganda and Tanzania are examples).[5]

The CAS as a key and visible strategic document is a relatively recent phenomenon, as country planning documents were formerly one of the Bank's most tightly held documents. Its current form and public disclosure emerged from sometimes difficult negotiations. Not surprisingly, candor has been a casualty of the evolving process and its public face, and the documents of today tend toward blandness, with striking similarities in language and issues among countries. CAS documents are prepared according to varying rhythms, with some updated every 3–5 years (the norm for the largest borrowers) and others after more lengthy interludes; CAS updates and interim reviews are increasingly used instead of a full update, especially when there is a protracted period of uncertainty (as, for example, in Kenya). The CAS process is demanding and costly, and country teams thus embark on the exercise with some reticence, but once it starts it tends to be all consuming for those involved. Many CAS documents, more in their process than tangible outcome, reflect new departures in World Bank relationships but the central idea is that the strategy is a living document, constantly updated and tweaked to reflect changing realities.

The Poverty Reduction Strategy Paper (PRSP)[6] relies on a separate strategic process, the primary differences being that the PRSP is designed to reflect the country's strategy whereas the CAS is the World Bank's own programming exercise. Nonetheless, the World Bank expects to see considerable synergy between a country's CAS and PRSP. PRSPs are prepared by countries which are part of the Highly Indebted Poor Countries (HIPC) initiative (see Chapter 7 for a discussion of its genesis and operation), whose central goal is to ensure that debt relief is explicitly tied to a strategic focus on poverty reduction. The PRSP is prepared by the government (often with support from the IMF and World Bank in various forms) and its partners, and is then reviewed by the IMF and World Bank, up to the level of their respective boards (based both on the PSRP documents and on a "Joint Advisory Note"). The process is tied directly to decisions on debt relief and to various concessional funding instruments of the IMF and World Bank. Some governments pursue similar strategic planning under a different name (so nomenclature can be confusing), or launch an interim PRSP process that, as the name suggests, involves less detail and usually more limited public participation. PRSPs are a focus of much attention and several reviews have highlighted the widely varying experience, ranging from meaningful and broad strategic engagement (Zambia and Tanzania are considered good examples by some) to more boilerplate exercises geared towards the critical facet of assuring release of badly needed funds.

The CAS (and in appropriate cases the PRSP) lays out dynamic and detailed plans for advice and lending from the Bank, supervision of the country's portfolio of policies and projects, and other World Bank-supported activities, as well as expected results and performance benchmarks. In addition to the core work of advice and lending, the World Bank program generally covers aid coordination, special topics and funds, training and capacity building, and other "services" that the World Bank can provide. The reviews of the CAS within the Bank would focus on different issues by country, but three common themes would be partnership arrangements (including notions of comparative advantage) with special focus on links to the IMF, different operational and lending scenarios and the "triggers"—that is, actions and events that might take Bank operations from a "low" to a "high" case, and how results will be measured and judged. Most contemporary strategies cover the World Bank Group, and thus outline activities by the International Finance Corporation (IFC) and Multilateral Investment Guarantee Agency (MIGA) (see Chapter 2), though often in less detail.

The World Bank provides continuous macroeconomic analysis for active countries (where the Bank has a significant program), punctuated by specific reports and less formal advisory notes. This reporting on country economies provides an underpinning for the Bank's analysis of different sectors within that country, and is designed both to tie the macroeconomic overview to specific investments and projects, and also to feed into its regional and global reporting systems. The profile of such analytic work (termed Analytic and Advisory Activities, or AAA) can and should be entirely tailor-made to the needs of individual countries, and thus varies widely. Two common examples—performed by multidisciplinary teams—are poverty assessments and public expenditure reviews. The trend is toward more participatory analysis with government and other partners, and more pragmatic, action-oriented analysis to support economic reforms or investment decisions. The Bank expects to share most such analyses with governments and more widely.

As noted, the CAS details plans for World Bank lending, whether involving financing from IBRD or IDA, or a blend. Most World Bank lending operations are relatively large and programmed several years in advance: the project cycle includes notional plans for succeeding operations and provides for their preparation, so the process is continuous. The lending program for most countries involves a mix of the many instruments that have emerged over the years. These range from relatively small pilot or capacity-building projects, to classic investments in specific programs such as road-building, to intermediary operations such as community development schemes or social action funds, to sector operations in health, education, power, or transport, to policy-support operations such as Development Policy Loans and Public Investment Support Credits. The ideal is a carefully crafted mix with strong links among the instruments and active efforts to harmonize financing from various development partners.

Each project is subject to continuous monitoring and support from the World Bank—a process termed supervision. Project teams normally report on progress twice a year, but a healthy recent trend is toward continuous supervision, often by teams based in the country, with their expertise reflecting the specific rhythms and needs of the borrower. When an operation comes to a close, the borrower and Bank staff prepare a completion note, that is reviewed by the Bank's Independent Evaluation Group (in varying degrees of detail). Supervision is a vital part of the World Bank's work, both because implementation of plans is where real benefits occur, and because such activity brings Bank staff into direct contact with daily realities. However, supervision work can be backbreaking, and the rewards less obvious than for work geared to developing and negotiating fresh new lending. While supervision deserves high priority and managerial attention, it has suffered from relative neglect for many years, and special efforts now emphasize reviewing portfolio performance and rewarding excellence with considerable fanfare.[7] Good supervision involves close relationships with the borrowing institutions, a clear understanding of the appropriate role for the Bank (as partner but not implementer), strong focus on proactive problem-solving, and continuous learning from experience and readiness to adapt and change to reflect both lessons and changing circumstances.

The CAS is supposed to serve as a dynamic guide to World Bank operations, shaped by changing circumstances and active learning from experience, and each CAS must include sections on lessons learned both from global experience and specific experience in that country. The Independent Evaluation Group often conducts specific reviews of country performance, and the continuing fodder of completion reports and supervision findings are supposed to inform both day-to-day experience and longer-term planning.

How does such a complex country program work in actual practice? Each country works with a country team—a term loosely applied to Bank staff members intensively involved in each country. In the matrix structure that is a deliberate part of the Bank's organizational design, teams form to meet specific needs, with a premium on bringing together locally based and international World Bank staff (the latter supposed to bring experience from across the world). The aspiration is that these multisectoral groups will work closely with their country counterparts on a continuing basis. However, vital as country teams are to delivering the coherent and creative program the Bank aspires to offer, mobilizing such teams can be extraordinarily challenging, given shifting assignments among staff members working in widely separated locations. This process accentuates the leadership, programming, and integration responsibilities of the country director, who plays a critical role in the contemporary World Bank. Teams work very differently from country to country, with superb examples contrasting with fragmented and even fractious arrangements.

Country work feeds into a vital, evolving, and sensitive Bank process of assessing each country's overall performance, which has direct repercussions for allocating resources, especially from IDA. The annual Country Policy and Institutional Assessment (CPIA) rates each IDA-eligible nation against a set of 16 criteria grouped into four clusters: economic management, structural policies, policies for social inclusion and equity, and public-sector management and institutions. The World Bank used to hold such judgments closely, but increasingly publicizes them, and thus they have implications well beyond the Bank, such as for investment ratings by credit rating agencies and individual investors.

This nuts-and-bolts description roughly outlines what is often a complex and creative mix of World Bank activities in each country. The Bank might also help coordinate aid (see Chapter 4, and examples in Chapter 5), provide small grants for a limited number of activities in specific sectors especially social and catalytic activities, and administer activities on behalf of other development partners.

Sectors, networks, and quality

Like all major organizations, especially those that work internationally, the World Bank faces continuous tension between a geographic approach, which focuses on a country and larger region and a sectoral approach, which concentrates on arenas such as education, urban development, and energy. This tension is particularly demanding for the World Bank because of its dual mandates to serve as a global institution, with a worldwide agenda, and its membership and governance structure, which accentuate its relationships with individual countries. While elements of both are always at work, the balance manifests itself as a moving pendulum, with the Bank sometimes focusing more on responding to the initiatives, wishes, and specific conditions of individual countries, and sometimes emphasizing a broader, thus more global perspective.

The World Bank's sector work has deep traditions going back to its earliest years, but today its terminology and ethos are driven largely by a 1997 reorganization that aimed to emphasize technical excellence with global reach. Toward that end, the Bank groups its sector work (and also a large part of its operational staff) into four broad networks: Poverty Reduction and Economic Management, Human Development, Sustainable Development, and Financial and Private Sector Development. Each network includes several specific sectors. For example, the Human Development network includes education, health, and social protection (which covers pensions, labor markets, social funds), while Sustainable Development encompasses energy, water, agriculture, environment, urban development, and social development. Each sector is led by a board that includes the managers who are assigned to work in specific regions plus an "anchor" unit working globally. The anchors—which are often the first point of entry to the World Bank for outsiders—have varying and not always precisely defined mandates to oversee staffing plans and performance, monitor cutting-edge developments in the field, and sustain the quality of operations. If, for example, an organization like Cooperative for Relief and Assistance Everywhere (CARE), the Global Fund for Women, or Coca Cola had an issue to discuss on education for girls or demobilization strategy across several countries, they would approach the Washington-based country anchors. If their focus is the Democratic Republic of the Congo or Honduras, they would normally be directed to the country office based in Kinshasa or Tegucigalpa.

For a time, the idea (which when implemented resulted in predictable chaos) was that country directors were responsible for strategies, relations, and above all budgets allocated to their country of responsibility, while sector directors managed staff and oversaw the quality of their work. The creative tension of matching one to the other was designed to produce creative synergy and respond to changing country realities. Following adjustments, the contemporary arrangements are more nuanced and often messy; thus an appreciation of the organizational philosophy that lies behind day-to-day life at the World Bank is often needed to understand who does what and why.

Today that philosophy focuses strongly on ensuring that the Bank's work is of high quality, and linking that work and resources to results. The Bank has created elaborate systems designed to achieve both ends. These include the CAS system, its links to continuous independent evaluation, the creative tension between country and sector teams, responsibility within networks and sectors for judging staff performance, and various mechanisms for seeking outside advice at many stages, which can include peer review for individual tasks, special advisory groups, and survey instruments. The Quality Assurance Group—a significant and relatively recent mechanism—attests to the strongly held view that quality is of paramount importance and is best achieved when integrated into operational work. That group has a mandate to conduct special reviews of projects it selects just after board approval, to judge what is seen as the critical element of "quality at entry." A parallel system responds to requests by managers for a "second opinion" from the group on challenging operations. Finally they conduct random reviews and an overall annual assessment of supervision performance to keep the focus on the effectiveness of project and program implementation.

Centralization versus decentralization also brings both philosophical and practical tensions. The World Bank historically was highly centralized, with decision-making concentrated at the top of the hierarchy and almost all staff based at the Washington DC headquarters. Most major decisions climbed the hierarchy to senior officials and the board. Today, the talk is of decentralization and "country-led" decision-making and a progressive steady increase in country offices marks important shifts in the balance of power. The Bank nonetheless has a somewhat schizophrenic quality, with marked rhetorical focus on decentralization, a reality that most day-to-day decisions in practice are made by operational staff, and a mystique of centralized and often rigid decision-making.

The World Bank's intellectual agenda

When asked to highlight the World Bank's primary contribution to development, most staff members would cite ideas and knowledge. The Bank has, increasingly over the years, come to see itself and to be seen as an intellectual leader that draws together many strands of development thinking. It aspires to be a leader particularly within the field of economics, to trace new paths, define the agenda on specific issues, and use this knowledge to advocate for development.

This list suggests some obvious tensions and questions: if the World Bank is an advocate, can it be an objective analyst? Are priorities for country and research work set by the agenda, or the agenda by experience? Who judges and assures quality? And how much is Bank thinking dominated by economics which is, going back to the Articles of Agreement but even more in practical organizational culture, the World Bank's leading discipline, and how effective is interdisciplinary work? The World Bank seeks to navigate these shoals with a bewildering array of efforts to gather data, conduct special studies, run consultations and conferences, publish findings, and train staff members and development actors. At its best, the Bank's research and policy work is truly outstanding—indeed, without parallel. The role and work do, however, face significant challenges, not least of which is finding a path through the maze of responsibilities and outputs. Coordination with other researchers (including those within other UN agencies) presents continuous challenges but, as in a university, there are ample opportunities for collaborative work and almost continuous conferences. Here, a priority for the Bank is to guard against the tendency for its contacts to be overly dominated by the developed world, and especially US-based institutions. For example, the Global Development Network (GDN), launched in 1997 by the World Bank to link research institutions across the world, was created to engage developing country institutions more actively; it is now an independent entity.[8]

The World Bank is plainly not a university, though it shares some characteristics with academic institutions, including considerable fragmentation among researchers and multiple agendas. The large research function, housed in many units, is led by a separate department under the World Bank's chief economist, who acts as one of the institution's senior leaders. It is noteworthy that the official intellectual leader is unambiguously an economist, underscoring the challenges the World Bank has long faced in ensuring a truly interdisciplinary focus, and integrating economic analysis with voluminous practical experience with projects and sectors. Also worth noting is the World Bank Institute (WBI), which began in the 1950s as a small unit offering courses to officials from developing countries, but today is aptly if informally described as the World Bank's university; it too sees itself as providing intellectual leadership in the development field. WBI aims to build capacity for development by offering both training and policy advice on managing economies and reducing poverty, environmentally and socially sustainable development, financial and private-sector development, governance, human development, and infrastructure (to name a few). WBI reaches out globally, inter alia, to parliamentarians, journalists, teachers, youth, and civil society leaders.

World Bank research is very much data driven, and increasingly geared toward what is termed global monitoring, with explicit ties to the Millennium Development Goals. It is also issue driven. Two annual reports reflect this focus. The first is the Global Monitoring Report, ambitiously described as "a framework for accountability in global development policy." The second is the World Development Report, produced each year since 1978, and each year focusing on a different topic. Table 3.1 lists recent WDR topics—an impressive cumulative listing of development issues. Two other annual flagship publications are *Global Development Finance* and *Global Economic Prospects*.

The Bank's research efforts yield a bewildering array of reports, and also underpin the organization's policy statements (including major speeches by the Bank president) and many publications, journals, and informal reports. The Bank also produces materials directed to schools, and has invested heavily in its web site to make it cutting edge. The "Prospects for Development" page offers access to information, analysis, and advice on global trends in the world economy, especially on trade, financial flows, and commodity prices, and the impact of those trends on developing countries. Created within the Bank but now a separate entity is the Development Gateway Foundation, which has created a Web portal for sharing information and knowledge on development worldwide (see more on this below).[9] The tools on this web site bring together people and organizations who are working to improve life in developing countries.

Navigating the organization

The World Bank can appear opaque to many outside and even inside the organization. An understanding of four elements can help people navigate the institution: its organizational bones; the practical implications of its governance structure for day-to-day work; the organizational culture and character of Bank staff; and the affiliate structure and its implications. Figure 3.1 shows a skeleton organization chart linking the major players. This should, even as a skeleton, be read with caution as there are fairly frequent changes in organization and the portfolios of the managing directors who report to the president. An example is recent changes in the line reporting arrangements for

Table 3.1 The focus of World Development Reports[1]

2009	Spatial Dimensions of Development
2008	Agriculture for Development
2007	Development and the Next Generation
2006	Equity and Development
2005	A Better Investment Climate for Everyone
2004	Making Services work for Poor People
2003	Sustainable Development in a Dynamic World
2002	Building Institutions for Markets
2000–2001	Attacking Poverty
1999–2000	Entering the 21st Century
1998–1999	Knowledge for Development
1997	The State in a Changing World
1996	From Plan to Market
1995	Workers in an Integrating World
1994	Infrastructure for Development
1993	Investing in Health
1992	Development and the Environment
1991	The Challenge of Development
1990	Poverty
1989	Financial Systems and Development
1988	Public Finance in Development
1987	Industrialization and Foreign Trade
1986	Trade and Pricing Policies in World Agriculture
1985	International Capital and Economic Development
1984	Population Change and Development
1983	Management and Development
1982	Agriculture and Economic Development
1981	National and International Adjustment
1980	Poverty and Human Development

Notes:
[1] Synopses available at http://web.worldbank.org/WBSITE/EXTERNAL/
EXTDEC/EXTRESEARCH/EXTWDRS/0,contentMDK:20227703~pagePK:
478093~piPK:477627~theSitePK:477624,00.html

both the officers responsible for external affairs (which includes the UN) and human development. What is perhaps most essential is to note the dotted lines of the various units that report to the board as their status and relationships differ markedly from those responsible directly to the president.

The ultimate authority for the World Bank is the Board of Governors. The Bank's governors—one appointed by each member government—normally meet annually (by tradition, two successive years in Washington, DC, and abroad each third year). The governors exercise their direct impact almost entirely through a defining Bank characteristic: its resident Board of Directors, which includes 24 members (each with

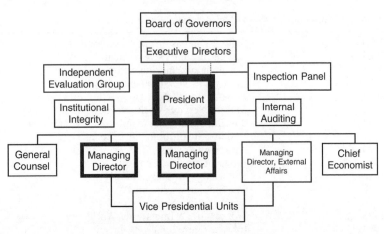

Figure 3.1 The World Bank's organization: the skeleton.

an alternate and a small staff of advisors and assistants). This board and its committees operate continuously, supported by the Secretary's Department. The governors are almost always officials from governments' finance departments, and they and the executive directors usually have training and experience in economics and finance; it is noteworthy how often their positions and approaches differ markedly from those of diplomats from the same countries, and from those of more multidisciplinary UN employees. The financial and economic focus of the Bank starts with its governors and board.

The workings of the board vary over time, but reflect two enduring tensions: first, between directors' responsibilities to their governments and to the World Bank; and second, between the board's responsibility for policy and management's responsibility for day-to-day operations. Two major shifts in the board's work have occurred in recent years. The board formerly focused on considering and approving each and every loan proposal. While the board still formally approves loans, attention has shifted toward reviewing policies and programs and special issues. And, for many years, especially during the Cold War, the board discussed matters in individual nations only gingerly and usually peripherally. Today detailed and frequent discussions of each country's strategies and policies are the board's central fare, requiring fancy footwork to tread carefully around the boundaries of topics with a clearly political character.

The board operates under two realities: first, the underlying fact of very different voting powers of each member, because of the weighted voting system (see Table 3.2); thus, as of mid-2007 the United States executive director cast 16.41 percent when votes were tallied, while one African executive director, representing 24 countries, cast 2 percent and China 2.79 percent (this for IBRD, as distinguished from IDA and IFC). And second, the strong tradition and practice of seeking consensus and assuring equal voice if not votes. This means that in practice votes are rarely taken and tabulated and a delicate and complex balance of power characterizes board dynamics.

The World Bank is very much a presidential institution, with the president exercising substantial authority by mandate (as chair of the board, and with significant power to appoint staff), and by setting a tone; the president is expected to provide strong leadership within the Bank and in the development community more broadly. The process of appointing a new president for the past several decades has evoked great concern and frustration, as it has been opaque and dependent in practice on an unvetted decision by the US president; though the board formally appoints the president, it has never directly contested a US nomination. The transition between James Wolfensohn, for ten years a driving and charismatic leader, and Paul Wolfowitz, who took office 1 June 2005, was particularly traumatic, partly because Wolfowitz's nomination caught many by surprise, but more so because the transition unrolled at a very slow pace, and above all because Wolfowitz failed patently to gain the trust of the institution's managers and staff, rarely even discussing issues and plans with them (see Chapter 2). The selection of Robert Zoellick as Paul Wolfowitz' successor in mid-2007 raised the familiar arguments—that the selection process should involve an open worldwide search for the best person available, but tradition prevailed and no serious political will was evident to contest the traditional "gentlemen's agreement" on the US prerogative to name the new president (linked to agreement that the European governments could designate the Managing Director of the IMF).

The current organizational structure is relatively straightforward, at least at the top, with managing directors, the chief economist, the secretary, the treasurer, the head of human resources, and the chief counsel reporting to the president. The two watchdog units—the Internal Evaluation Group and the Inspection Panel (IP)—report directly to the board. Vice presidents, who shoulder major responsibility for day-to-day work and report to the president through the managing directors, fall into three main groups. These include the regional vice presidents, who lead large staffs working directly on countries; the network vice presidents, who are responsible for the technical and sector operations; and an array of supporting vice presidents,

Table 3.2 Governance and power: voting rights in IBRD, IDA, and IFC

Country or Country Group[1]	IBRD Voting Share (percent)	IDA Voting Share (percent)	IFC Voting Share (percent)
United States*	16.41	13.01	23.67
Japan*	7.87	10.11	5.88
Germany*	4.49	6.49	5.37
France*	4.31	5.15	5.04
United Kingdom*	4.31	4.14	5.04
Belgian chair** (10 countries, Europe, Turkey)	4.81	4.64	5.20
Mexican Chair** (9 countries from Latin America plus Spain)	4.50	2.22	4.05
Netherlands Chair** (13 countries, Europe plus Israel)	4.47	3.90	3.63
Canada Chair** (14 countries, Canada, Caribbean countries plus Ireland)	3.85	4.38	3.86
Brazil Chair** (9 countries, Latin America, Haiti plus Philippines)	3.56	3.02	3.16
Italy Chair** (8 countries from Southern Europe plus Timor Leste)	3.51	3.40	4.23
South Korea Chair** (14 countries, East Asia including Australia, Pacific Islands)	3.45	3.24	3.05
India Chair** (5 countries, South Asia)	3.40	4.19	4.12

Ethiopia Chair** (22 countries, Anglo-phone, Lusophone Africa)	3.36	4.58	2.40
Norway Chair** (9 countries, Scandinavia)	3.34	5.16	3.6
Pakistan Chair** (8 countries, Maghreb, Iran, South Asia, Ghana)	3.19	2.20	1.91
Switzerland Chair** (9 countries, south central Europe, Central Asia)	3.04	3.82	2.60
Kuwait Chair** (14 countries, Middle East Region)	2.91	2.26	1.43
China Chair** (1 country, China)	2.79	2.00	1.03
Saudi Arabia Chair** (1 country, Saudi Arabia)	2.79	3.36	1.26
Russia** (1 country, Russia)	2.79	0.31	3.39
Malaysia Chair** (11 South East Asian countries)	2.54	2.83	2.49
Argentina Chair** (6 South American countries)	2.32	1.61	2.66
Mauritius Chair** (24 African countries)	2.00	3.93	0.95

Source: IBRD, May 2007.

Notes:

* Appointed.

** Elected by country grouping.

[1] Executive Directors for the five largest shareholders are appointed by that shareholder and thus represent that single country; other executive directors are elected by groups of countries and represent country groupings which are voluntarily formed and can change, though they have traditionally been stable. The country listed as holding the executive director chair is as of mid-2007. Country groupings are for IBRD and differ somewhat for IDA and IFC.

including finance, human resources, research, and technology. Under vice presidents come directors. The roles and responsibilities of country directors—most of whom are based outside the United States—are reasonably clear and prominent: they determine relationships and often programs within individual countries. The roles of sector directors are less clear, varying by network and over time. At the base—but most critical in terms of real impact—are operational staff, many of whom carry the title of task team leader, meaning that they have at least some responsibility for managing individual activities, or tasks.

This orderly hierarchy is complicated by the organization's matrix structure (wherein most staff have dual responsibility to technical and country managers), which is designed to ensure flexibility and adaptation in response to changing circumstances. The hierarchy is also complicated by an extraordinary array of programs reflected in small organizational units, some partially spun off from the Bank, some masked within departments. Examples include the GDN, Global Development Gateway (GDG), GEF and CGAP.

The World Bank staff and organizational culture

So who is the World Bank? Its staff is and needs to be in many respects its strongest asset, as the World Bank is truly a "knowledge institution." Highly educated (large numbers with PhDs and other advanced degrees), with a broad range of experience, multinational (representing some 120 nations), multidisciplinary, motivated, determined, optimistic, self-confident, and sometimes arrogant are descriptive terms that come readily to mind. Table 3.3 and Figures 3.2 and Figure 3.3 provide a thumbnail sketch of how the staff of the World Bank are allocated, and their concentration working on different regions, especially what is by far the most demanding continent, Africa. In terms of their physical location, this is changing fairly significantly and about 40 percent now live in developing countries.

Employment at the Bank is justly competitive, both because the work is so important and fascinating and because the salary structure is designed to be internationally competitive. Many thousand applications arrive each year, in contrast to only a few hundred permanent hires annually. The Young Professionals Program recruits each year a small group of superbly qualified young people to work at the Bank, after they are screened by several layers of staff. Most other recruitment occurs for specific positions, with sector boards reviewing applicants to assure fungibility and adherence to standards, and that the best person available is recruited for a job.

Table 3.3 The World Bank staff—some numbers

Total WBG staff (FY06)*:	10,854	
Average age	*FY05*	*FY06*
IBRD staff:	44.7	44.9
IFC staff:	41.8	41.5
MIGA staff:	43.9	43.8
Average tenure (yrs)	*FY05*	*FY06*
IBRD staff:	9.5	9.7
IFC staff:	7.5	7.2
MIGA staff:	8.3	8.3

Source: World Bank, end of August 2006.

Note:
Total Staff defined as open-ended and fixed term; excludes several categories of staff and temporary employees.

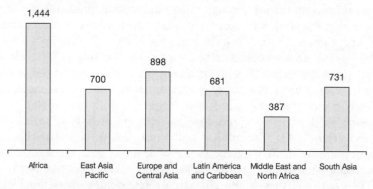

Figure 3.2 World Bank staff working on regions.

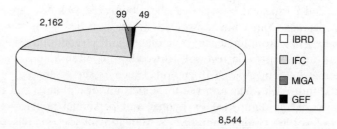

Figure 3.3 World Bank staff by Bank Group Institution.

Diversity has long been an issue and a challenge. The almost all white-male World Bank of the 1960s has given way to a much more diverse staff profile, but habits are sticky, and senior representation of women, Africans, and Japanese, to cite three prominent examples, is still below levels that demography and the substantive demands of the work touching these groups would suggest. Another unsurprising but note-worthy feature of the World Bank is its wide use of consultants, to fill gaps in expertise and carry out work during periods of peak workload. With high barriers to hiring designed to ensure open competition and maintain high standards, in practice consultants and other temporary assignments tend to be overused, leading to a sometimes disgruntled group of people aspiring for regular status but unable to break through.

Managing this international staff is no easy feat. The Bank of the past was a career institution, where people worked for many years and left very reluctantly, partly because they sought to retain their benefits and US visas but also because their families had put down roots. Staff were trained on the job through intense mentoring, gradually donning leadership responsibility. New employees absorbed the complex array of operational policies—which were not even collected in a single place—through a process akin to osmosis. The flip side was that many staff lost technical skills with time, and became somewhat jaded and complacent. The picture today is very different, with far higher, delib-erately encouraged staff turnover, and a high proportion of staff with limited Bank experience and growing numbers of outside recruits at management levels. The result is both creative and somewhat chaotic, as newly hired staff with the barest of training and oversight often negotiate with country officials and partners. The challenge is partly recognized, and new training programs and clearer operational gui-dance are among the reforms designed to ensure high standards for both work and behavior.

The World Bank's organizational culture is demanding (described once as "slash and burn" to reflect the cut and parry of internal criti-cism), and permeated by what can be a blinkered technical approach and resistance to new ideas, especially from "outside." Some resulting characteristics are a tendency to acronyms and jargon, and a surpris-ing but understandable recourse to worthy but often bland language reflecting the "objective of the month," such as sustainability, partici-pation, and results. The appetite for good multidisciplinary and cross-cutting work is dampened by budget and personnel policies, which tend to favor less complex approaches. Management selection has always been problematic, despite quite elaborate systems now in place for careful vetting of candidates by broadly based committees; nonetheless the

Bank faces the familiar yet significant challenges of a tendency to risk aversion in managerial appointments and sometimes may favor "safe" candidates with technical qualifications rather than those with the kind of broad-based savvy and compassion that development work demands.

Bank staff tend to complain, and exuberant, unqualified support for any person or policy is rare. A glimpse of the Bank's cultural failings—a wonderful tribute to self-criticism—is the annual April 1 spoof publication *Bankswirled* (the authors' identities are a carefully guarded secret).[10] The Bank's internal complaint systems (*sui generis* to the Bank, because its international character generally bars recourse to country grievance and legal systems) are complex, and reflect well the difficult task of managing a diverse and demanding staff. These systems include ombudsmen who seek to work out solutions to problematic personnel situations, an internal Appeals Committee that hears cases and advises management on suggested remedies, and a formal Administrative Tribunal with binding authority.

The bottom line, nonetheless, is that the World Bank staff is made up of many remarkable people—professional, dedicated, diverse, demanding of themselves and others, hardworking, and above all dedicated to the mission of working for "a world free of poverty." Not all staff are excellent (though they might dispute that judgment) and the Bank faces long-standing difficulties in moving staff whose performance is mediocre or matching the right people to the right jobs. On balance, though, the World Bank has an excellent record of staff performance and service. Most important, it aspires to the highest standards of integrity and technical excellence.

Look to the money

Financial management is a major strength of the World Bank, reflecting 60-year-deep roots. (Chapter 2 briefly introduced the institution's financial structure and financial challenges.) The Bank invests its reserves and pension fund, raises money on capital markets, negotiates for government contributions, above all for IDA, and oversees the financial dimensions of its large lending portfolio. It has also, increasingly and not without difficulty, been called upon to manage a wide array of trust funds on behalf of governments and other institutions. Three special features of this overall arena are worth highlighting: the sheer scope of the World Bank's financial operations and their growing diversity; its welcoming and emphasis on socially responsible investment; and challenges in managing the trust funds. (Later chapters will address two other important issues: countries' debt, and financial integrity and approaches to corruption.)

IBRD currently borrows around US$10–15 billion annually in about 11 currencies. It has offered IBRD bonds and notes in more than 48 currencies, in so doing opening up new markets for international investors in a variety of currencies. The World Bank's treasury is an extensive user of interest rate and currency swaps, with about US$30 billion in annual volume and a swap book totaling around US$150 billion. In its asset management business, the Bank now manages between US$60 and US$65 billion in global liquidity—cash on hand, held in portfolios and balanced funds for the World Bank Group, the staff pension fund, central banks, and other multilateral organizations. Finance ministries, central banks, and pension funds in various countries seek the Bank's technical assistance in developing strategies for managing assets and liabilities and building institutional capacity. In short, the World Bank has achieved a global reputation as a prudent and innovative borrower, investor, and risk manager, and that is a vital ingredient in its success. It has been called upon to provide fee-based services in these areas.

The World Bank today is preoccupied with its social responsibilities in numerous dimensions, including the social impact of its work and its sensitivity to social justice and policy issues (see Chapter 6). A subset of these issues permeates financial operations, and the Bank seeks to ensure that it "walks the talk" by providing leadership on socially responsible investing. This issue is likely to grow in importance as the diverse strands of the Bank's engagement in sustainability and social responsibility—including the IFC Equator Principles (see Chapter 4), advice on global warming, approaches to indigenous peoples, and gender policies—come into contact with areas like finance.

Over time, and in almost unperceived increments, the World Bank has taken on responsibility for managing an extraordinary array of special funds in trust: from $3 billion in 2000 to more than $21 billion in 2007. Accounted for separately from the Bank's own resources, these trust funds are financial and administrative arrangements with external donors that lead to grants for development needs considered to merit high priority, such as technical assistance, advisory services, debt relief, post-conflict transition, and co-financing. These trust funds help the Bank leverage its poverty reduction programs by funding operations where Bank resources are insufficient, help promote innovation, and allow the Bank to operate in unusual circumstances (for example, in disaster situations that require rapid mobilization, and in disputed situations such as Palestine and Iraq). Trust funds allow the Bank to forge new partnerships, such as with foundations and private companies. The issue is that management practices have not fully kept up with the explosion of trust funds as reporting and planning systems do not take them fully into account and, as a result, they are often less visible and less involved in incentives structures. Further, the special-purpose funds often compete with IDA in practice as they look to the same funding sources among the richer member governments.

Internal watchdogs

Who judges how the World Bank is doing? This has long sparked probing and contentious discussion, reflecting the notion that a self-critical culture is essential to assure both learning and accountability; debate about whether the evaluation functions truly belong within the institution or should be more independent; and the introduction of mechanisms to allow recourse in the event of harm caused through World Bank operations. In this connection, the Independent Evaluation Group (IEG)—a unit within the World Bank reporting directly to the Board of Executive Directors—plays a key role. The newer (12-year-old) IP has a less straightforward but also important place. Debate nonetheless continues as to whether these arms'-length but still internal evaluation mechanisms are sufficient to the task.

The IEG is a large department staffed by regular Bank employees and consultants, with a leader appointed with special provisions to ensure that he or she has independence despite working with and inside the World Bank (the five-year appointment is a career cap, i.e. the last job someone can hold at the Bank, and the board evaluates the IEG director). Formerly known as the Operations Evaluation Department, IEG was created in 1973, and undertakes a wide variety of tasks hammered out with the board. The IEG's mandate is broad: to assess what works, and what does not; how projects are planned, run, and sustained; and the lasting contribution of the Bank to a country's overall development. The goal is to learn from experience, provide an objective basis for assessing the results of the Bank's work, and provide accountability in achieving its objectives. Most IEG work is now public, with a wide array of reports available on its web site.[11]

The IP was established in 1993 to address the concerns of people who might be affected by Bank projects, and to ensure that the Bank adheres to its operational policies and procedures while designing, preparing, and implementing projects. The panel consists of three members appointed by the board for non-renewable five-year terms. Its caseload obviously varies, but has included projects on most continents. The most prominent and controversial was the Western China Rural Development Project, which ensnared the Bank in a complex controversy involving the government of China and activists on behalf of Tibet. Detailed review by the panel in 1999—2000 highlighted instances where indeed the World Bank had not followed all of its own policies and procedures designed to assure both environmental and social standards, but it also highlighted the complexity of development challenges. The upshot was that China decided to halt the process of World Bank funding and proceeded to implement the project without outside financial assistance.

The IP represents an interesting approach to "accountability from below," as it gives to some of those who are presumed to benefit or are otherwise affected by World Bank-funded projects the right to trigger an investigation into unplanned negative outcomes. As such, the IP complements the Bank's other accountability mechanisms, like IEG, that are triggered "from above," i.e., by those who fund a particular action and seek to know whether planned investment objectives have been achieved. The IP gives direct voice and access to those harmed or in fear of being harmed. After trying unsuccessfully to solve their problems with the Bank's management, they can bring their concerns directly (and often confidentially) to the Panel and through that avenue to the Bank's governing structure. Requests for inspection usually come from groups of people who feel that they are being harmed or will be harmed by Bank investments.

Also worth note is that the IP focus is the Bank, not the borrower (i.e., country). The inspection focuses on whether any of the perceived or actual harms are related to the Bank's failures in complying with its own policies and procedures as it supports the design and implementation of projects and programs. Inspections thus target the Bank, not host institutions. Equally important, the IP does not criticize the actions and decisions of individual staff members but those of the Bank as an institution.

Civil Society was a major force in establishing the IP and continues to be a major supporter because they see the Panel as a way for the Bank to practice what it preaches—thus to give voice to the poor and those often excluded from the development process. NGOs see the IP as a key instrument for ensuring that policies they have fought hard for are truly implemented. The Bank's board views the IP as an important tool for discharging their supervisory duties and for minimizing reputational risks for the Bank. Independence and impartiality are two important IP hallmarks. The IP reports to the board but without direct interference so it enjoys complete independence. IP members have no former employment affiliation with the Bank and are barred from employment or other commercial relations with the Bank after their five-year non-renewable term. Potential drawbacks are that the threat of IP appeals can make the Bank's work more cumbersome but the policies concerned are an essential part of the Bank's contemporary role. Safeguard policies may be complex and need adapting but in whatever form they exist, they need to be complied with. The IP adds no new burdens but is a fact-finding body to establish whether these policies were complied with by the Bank.

The Panel's creation and its work manifest an increasing global concern with "compliance." The World Bank IP was the first institution of this kind, but it has since been replicated in all the other international and regional development banks (most recently the African Development Bank). Other development assistance organizations are considering similar mechanisms. While case numbers have increased in recent years (probably as the IP becomes better known), it is to the credit of the Bank that relatively few projects have been subjected to a full IP investigation. As of June 2007, the panel had been presented with 46 cases.[12]

Portrait in facts and figures

Several classic measures of the World Bank's work are the most commonly cited statistical measures of the World Bank, though they tend to overplay the lending and financial aspects of its role, in contrast to the ideas and advice dimensions (obviously much harder to show in tables). The basic portrait of Bank lending and operations is summarized below along these lines.

The first measure is the World Bank's historic portfolio—aggregate lending by region, country, subject, and theme over time. Box 3.1 shows this portrait in summary form. There are many messages beyond the increase in aggregate lending, but the details of year to year, country to country, and sector to sector variations tend to be rather masked in the broad numbers.

The second measure is the snapshot of World Bank operations for a given year. Figure 3.4 shows this profile for the fiscal year 2007, showing how new lending was divided by region. The table above all highlights the different profiles of the different regions, including Africa's almost total reliance on IDA resources and the blended picture for the largest lending regions of South Asia and Latin America.

A third measure is a first effort to approach results, in this instance measured in disbursements (as opposed to the commitments reflected in the new lending).

Box 3.1   **The World Bank's historical portfolio**

(a) Total lending (over institutions' history) (US$ millions, as of 30 June 2007)

IBRD	IDA
433,000	181,000

(b) Total portfolio (disbursed and outstanding) (US$ millions, as of 30 June 2007)

IBRD	IDA	IFC
97,805	102,457	25,400*

Note:
Committed portfolio excludes $5.5 billion in syndicated loans.

(c) Annual lending total, FY1997–2007 (US$ millions, data as of 30 June 2007)

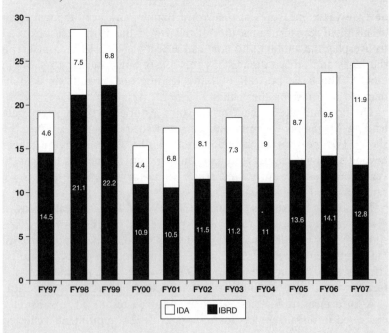

(d) Annual disbursements, FY1997–2007 (US$ millions, data as of 30 June 2007)

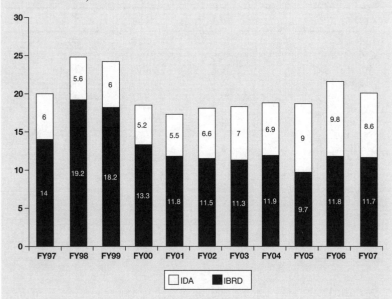

(e) Annual lending by major sectors FY05–07 (US$ millions)

	FY05	*FY06*	*FY07*
Agriculture, Fishing, and Forestry	1,933.6	1,751.9	1,717.4
Education	1,951.1	1,990.6	2,021.8
Energy and Mining	1,822.7	3,030.3	1,784.0
Finance	1,675.1	2,319.7	1,613.6
Health and Other Social Services	2,216.4	2,132.3	2,752.5
Industry and Trade	1,629.4	1,542.2	1,181.3
Information and Communication	190.9	81.0	148.8
Law and Justice and Public Administration	5,569.3	5,857.6	5,468.2
Transportation	3,138.2	3,214.6	4,949.0
Water, Sanitation, and Flood Protection	2,180.2	1,721.0	3,059.4
Sector Total	*22,307.0*	*23,641.2*	*24,695.8*
Of which IBRD	13,611.0	14,135.0	12,825.8
Of which IDA	8,696.1	9,506.2	11,866.9

(f) Historic lending to 15 largest borrowers (total new commitments over time) (US$ billions, as of 30 June 2007)

Country	IBRD	IDA	Total
India	35.1	34.3	69.4
China	32.6	10	42.6
Brazil	38.2	0	38.2
Mexico	38.1	0	38.1
Indonesia	30.1	2.5	32.6
Turkey	26.2	0.2	26.4
Argentina	24.5	0	24.5
Pakistan	7.4	10.3	17.7
South Korea	15.5	0.1	15.6
Colombia	14.5	0.02	14.5
Russian Federation	13.7	0	13.7
Philippines	12.3	0.3	12.6
Bangladesh	0.05	12.4	12.5
Nigeria	6.3	3.6	9.9
Morocco	9.7	0.05	9.8

(g) IBRD and IDA lending by type of lending instrument in FY 2007*

Lending instrument	IBRD lending (in US$ billions)	IBRD projects	IDA lending (in US$ billions)	IDA projects
Investment lending	9.2	90	9.3	154
Development policy lending	3.6	22	2.6	35
Total	12.8	112	11.9	189

Notes:
* Investment lending includes: Adaptable Program Loan (APL), Emergency Recovery Loan (ERL), Financial Intermediary Loan (FIL), Learning and Innovation Loan (LIL), Specific Investment Loan (SIL), Sector Investment and Maintenance Loan (SIM), Technical Assistance Loan (TAL).

(h) Post-conflict grants

	FY 98–00	FY01	FY02	FY03	FY04	FY05	FY06
Grants ($ millions)	20	15.2	12.7	13.4	5.2	6.0	11.7
Number of Grants	55	26	26	22	16	12	14

Note:
Major FY06 post-conflict grants included: Russia ($2.1 million), Nigeria ($1.8 million), Philippines ($1.5 million), Haiti ($1.2 million), Iraq ($.7 million), and Africa, regional ($2.0 million)

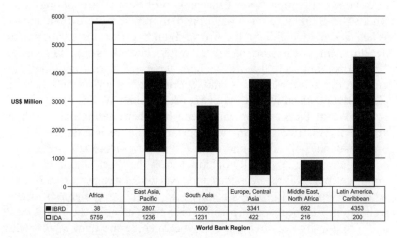

Figure 3.4 World Bank lending by region (Fiscal 07).

Summary

The Bank's operational ideals, the long-term nature of its country engagement, and the interlocking aspects of the Bank's different program elements (notably lending, advice, technical support, training, and aid coordination) are illustrated through a fictional country, Utania, which begins as a very poor newly independent country, uses its aid partners exceptionally well, and attains the status of a middle income country that has little need for Bank support after some 20 years. The ideal is, of course, rarely if ever attained, and most country partnerships involving the Bank mix good and bad practice and go through very different phases, and show different emphases and practical relationships. The CAS is a key instrument for planning and exploring how the Bank can support a country and it describes broad objectives, specific operational plans (loans, credits, criteria for aid levels, governance indicators, gaps in knowledge, and relationships within the aid community). The CAS and PRSP have different roles, with the PRSP tied explicitly to debt relief, but both highlight the focus on articulating poverty strategies and enhancing aid levels and partnerships. Relationships with individual countries are the heart of World Bank operations, and vary significantly, especially in line with the country's level of poverty and need for concessional assistance and its institutional capacity. The Bank's focus is the poorest countries, especially Africa, though its operations in middle income countries are also large and important. Especially problematic are failing states where the Bank is often ill-equipped to provide more than advice. When asked to highlight the World Bank's primary contribution to development, most staff members would cite ideas and knowledge. The Bank's intellectual work includes large and varied activities ranging from country analysis and specific, often informal advice to global data collection and major reports like the WDR.

The World Bank's organization can be a bewildering maze of hierarchies and matrices, making it important to appreciate the underlying organizational philosophy and culture. The governance structures, especially the weighted voting that characterizes the World Bank, also have important practical repercussions and give special weight to relationships with the board and progress towards the Bank's stated goal of decentralization. Finance, not surprisingly, is a focal area for the World Bank and a major area of strength. Activities include the Bank's borrowing programs, management of its assets, efforts to enhance the social responsibility of its investments and portfolio, and increasing acceptance of responsibility for managing trust funds on behalf of other institutions.

Evaluation and accountability for results are major areas of focus for the World Bank. Two internal but independent entities carry a large share of the burden for such evaluation: the IEG and the IP. The story of the Bank can also be told in numbers, though these tend to focus primarily on lending and disbursement volumes, and less on the vital element of ideas, advice and capacity building. In short, the World Bank's work is complex, interlocking, and varies widely by country and time period. At its best, it is a favored and effective partner in mobilizing development support, experience, and ideas.

4 Development partnerships and the World Bank

The contemporary World Bank is an integral part of the complex international development arrangements sometimes loosely called the aid community. Within this complex and fast-changing world, the Bank is quite often called upon as a leader, while in other situations it follows the lead of other agencies or, most significantly, the responsible governments. The "architecture," that is, the overall structure of the arrangements, is manifestly increasing in complexity so that a general consensus has formed that the system is unmanageable, broken in many respects, and in need of reform. This applies both at the international, global level, where a particular recent focus is concern at the proliferation of "vertical" funds that focus on specific issues (like HIV/AIDS and malaria), and at country level, where a long tradition of aid coordination arrangements has deeply engaged the World Bank.

Beyond the dynamics and mechanisms of the overall aid system, the World Bank operates through a vast array of specific partnership arrangements, and there are few if any activities that do not involve working affiliations with other organizations. Partnerships start close to home with the Bank's own affiliates (International Finance Corporation (IFC), Multilateral Investment Guarantee Agency (MIGA), International Center for the Settlement of Investment Disputes (ICSID)) and organizations housed under the Bank's own roof (Global Environment Facility (GEF), Consultative Group to Assist the Poor (CGAP), and Consultative Group on International Agricultural Research (CGIAR), for example) as well as a category sometimes referred to as "spin-offs"—organizations that began as part of the World Bank but are now independent entities (Global Development Network (GDN), Global Development Gateway (GDG), World Faiths Development Dialogue (WFDD) are examples). The Bank has complex and often quite different relationships with many if not most

UN agencies, beginning with its Bretton Woods sibling, the International Monetary Fund (IMF), and including the United Nations (UN) Secretariat organizations and most specialized UN agencies (United Nations Children's Fund (UNICEF), for example). The Bank cooperates with other international financial institutions (IFIs), notably the regional development banks and export credit agencies. It works closely with most bilateral aid agencies, with civil society organizations of many stripes, with foundations (including the largest among them, the Bill and Melinda Gates Foundation, but also with many others), private companies and business associations, academic institutions, and some private philanthropists. As in the case of the overall aid architecture, many argue that the arrangements have become far too complex, yet the dynamic producing the multiplication of partnerships nonetheless maintains a powerful momentum.

This chapter explores some of the issues involved in aid partnerships, and the Bank's roles in aid mobilization and harmonization. It looks first at the overall aid systems, including specific recent efforts to bring more focus and harmony and ease the burdens of management that fall on aid recipients, and then at country aid coordination mechanisms. It then turns to the World Bank itself, sketching a map of the different institutional partnerships in which it is engaged. Finally, it comments on the roles and responsibilities that go with the World Bank's global leadership and spokesperson role, sometimes termed the bully pulpit that the World Bank occupies. It bears note that several other books in the Global Institutions series also address the large elephant of aid mobilization and coordination from the perspectives of different organizations.

The aid mobilization and harmonization challenge

The layers of institutional relationships, alliances, partnerships, and overlap in the development field have become steadily more complex over the years. Dynamic partnership arrangements bringing in new actors especially from the private sector and civil society are transforming development work and bring new resources and creative synergies; they are also creating challenges to be inclusive and to share information more widely and clearly. The Millennium UN Summit in 2000 and the ensuing elaboration of the Millennium Development Goal (MDG) challenges and framework also has put a renewed and tangible focus on long-standing targets for increasing available development aid and on the goal of making international assistance more effective. The G8 (leaders of the eight largest world economies) has over the past decades played an increasingly active role especially in advancing the consensus on debt relief and pressing for higher aid levels.

Seen from many perspectives—but above all, that of a financial official leading development programs in an active country—the array of assistance programs and actors can be overwhelming. Good intentions and good will have produced a mish-mash, or a crazy quilt of overlapping systems and programs, with differing objectives, roles, financial arrangements, reporting procedures, and even underlying philosophies. Figure 4.1 offers a graphic illustration of the crazy quilt of different aid programs, replete with acronyms, working in a single African country.

There are different ways to look at this proliferation of aid programs and agencies. For most observers, especially those who have worked with country officials and tried to navigate the maze of different procedures and processes, the need for reform seems urgent and obvious. One key actor observed at a recent conference that it is time to "get a grip." New actors are coming onto the scene, making coordination still more difficult: China and India are the largest of those seen as "new" aid donors (though they have operated programs for many years) but others include several Eastern European countries

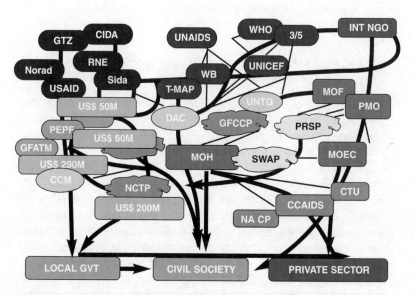

Figure 4.1 HIV/AIDS stakeholders and donors in one African country.

and countries like Brazil and Venezuela; most have not been part of the emerging consensus and coordination agreements and mechanisms. A significant minority of actors and observers, in contrast, celebrate the competition that characterizes the present system, the virtues of choice, and the enforced discipline that come about in an entrepreneurial and competitive environment. The reality is that no amount of coordination will bring total order to the system and indeed the advent of many new actors brings fresh visions and energy to the development business. However, this market-based spirit and the virtues of diversity do not obviate the large practical problems facing current systems and the need for reform.

The World Bank enters this fray from many directions. It has been a key player for some decades in the effort to encourage aid coordination and harmonization, and, especially since the 2002 Monterrey Financing for Development Summit, has worked closely with other partners (especially the Organisation for Economic Co-operation and Development (OECD) and Development Assistance Committee (DAC)) to forge an operational consensus behind principles of aid harmonization. These are reflected in two declarations, which emerged from conferences in 2003 in Rome and 2006 in Paris. Box 4.1 includes part of the Rome declaration of principles, which were made more specific with the Paris Declaration in March 2005, which involved over one hundred ministers, heads of agencies and officials.[1]

Box 4.1 **Extracts from the Rome Declaration on Aid Harmonization**

We, the heads of multilateral and bilateral development institutions and representatives of the IMF, other multilateral financial institutions, and partner countries gathered in Rome, Italy, on February 24–25, 2003, reaffirm our commitment to eradicating poverty, achieving sustained economic growth, and promoting sustainable development as we advance to an inclusive and equitable global economic system. Our deliberations are an important international effort to harmonize the operational policies, procedures, and practices of our institutions with those of partner country systems to improve the effectiveness of development assistance, and thereby contribute to meeting the Millennium Development Goals (MDGs). They directly support the broad agreement of the international development community on this issue as reflected in the Monterrey

Consensus (Report of the International Conference on Financing for Development, March 2002, para. 43). We express our appreciation to the governments of Jamaica, Vietnam, and Ethiopia, and to the bilateral donors and international institutions that sponsored and coordinated regional workshops in Kingston, Hanoi, and Addis Ababa in January 2003, in preparation for the Rome Forum. The key principles, lessons, and messages synthesized in the reports of these workshops have provided valuable input to the Forum ...

We agree that, for both donors and partner countries, the progress we make on the ground in programs and projects will be a concrete and important measure of the success of our efforts. We recognize that such progress can be facilitated and enhanced by harmonization efforts at the international and regional levels. Building on the work of the DAC/OECD and MDB working groups and on country experience, including the recent country initiatives, we commit to the following activities to enhance harmonization:

- Ensuring that development assistance is delivered in accordance with partner country priorities, including poverty reduction strategies and similar approaches, and that harmonization efforts are adapted to the country context.
- Reviewing and identifying ways to amend, as appropriate, our individual institutions' and countries' policies, procedures, and practices to facilitate harmonization. In addition, we will work to reduce donor missions, reviews, and reporting, streamline conditionalities, and simplify and harmonize documentation.
- Implementing progressively – building on experiences so far and the messages from the regional workshops – the good practice standards or principles in development assistance delivery and management, taking into account specific country circumstances. We will disseminate the good practices (synthesized in Annex A) to our managers and staff at headquarters and in country offices and to other in-country development partners.
- Intensifying donor efforts to work through delegated cooperation at the country level and increasing the flexibility of country-based staff to manage country programs and projects more effectively and efficiently.

- Developing, at all levels within our organizations, incentives that foster management and staff recognition of the benefits of harmonization in the interest of increased aid effectiveness.
- Providing support for country analytic work in ways that will strengthen governments' ability to assume a greater leadership role and take ownership of development results. In particular, we will work with partner governments to forge stronger partnerships and will collaborate to improve the policy relevance, quality, delivery, and efficiency of country analytic work.
- Expanding or mainstreaming country-led efforts (whether begun in particular sectors, thematic areas, or individual projects) to streamline donor procedures and practices, including enhancing demand-driven technical cooperation. The list of countries presently involved includes Ethiopia, Jamaica, Vietnam, Bangladesh, Bolivia, Cambodia, Honduras, Kenya, Kyrgyz Republic, Morocco, Niger, Nicaragua, Pacific Islands, Philippines, Senegal, and Zambia.
- Providing budget, sector, or balance of payments support where it is consistent with the mandate of the donor, and when appropriate policy and fiduciary arrangements are in place. Good practice principles or standards – including alignment with national budget cycles and national poverty reduction strategy reviews – should be used in delivering such assistance.
- Promoting harmonized approaches in global and regional programs.

The Paris Declaration[2] was seen as going beyond general principles to lay down a practical, action-orientated roadmap to improve the quality of aid and its impact on development. It highlighted 56 partnership commitments organized around the five key principles of ownership (by the country), alignment (of programs), harmonization (of procedures), managing for results (to enhance quality), and mutual accountability (within the aid community). It set out 12 indicators of aid effectiveness (with year 2010 targets for 11 of them) as a way of tracking and encouraging progress against the broader set of partnership commitments. More broadly, it promotes a model of partnership that improves transparency and accountability on the use of development resources.

Several recurring themes underlie these global efforts. The first (discussed in Chapter 7) is mobilizing the financial resources needed to attain the MDGs by showing more effectively that funds are well applied to poverty objectives. The second is to reduce the horrible inefficiencies, documented in excruciating detail in many documents, among them the running "killer statistics" tally of the Overseas Development Institute in London (among others cited are the following: 17 major official donors provide aid to Ghana's health system, all with different priorities and strategies, not including foundations, pharmaceutical industry projects and nongovernmental organization (NGOs);[3] WHO has 4600 separate agreements with donors and has to provide 1400 reports to donors each year;[4] Egypt has 22 donors in the health sector; 80 percent of the 80,000 aid projects underway at any one time (in 2005) were for less than $1 million;[5] 28 UN agencies were working on water in 2005; St Vincent—an island state with a population of 117,000—was asked to monitor 191 indicators on HIV/AIDS, while Guyana was asked to report on 169 indicators).[6] Third, it responds to specific plaints of country finance ministers about several burdens including the erratic timing, unpredictability, and clumsy forms in which aid is often delivered, including the very practical burden of multiple missions: a 14-country survey by the OECD and the World Bank showed an average of 200 donor missions per year, three-quarters of these by a handful of donors (the "chronic travelers"). Cambodia and Vietnam received 400 missions each, Nicaragua 289, Bolivia 270, Bangladesh 250.[7] Fourth, it addresses the common concern for linking aid to poverty objectives and governance reforms to aid management. Finally, it reflects a commendable effort to make the whole process more transparent and to allow much better information sharing.

Global roles and aid partnerships

The World Bank participates in a wide array of global events, starting within the UN system but also including the G8 and regional mechanisms like Asia-Pacific Economic Cooperation (APEC) meetings. The annual report to the Economic and Social Council of the UN offers the opportunity to pull together threads of development issues. The World Bank has offices (though small ones) in New York and Geneva, which represent the World Bank at the host of UN meetings that take place on a daily basis. These involve the specialized UN agencies (the Food and Agriculture Organization (FAO), the International Labour Organization (ILO)) meetings, major global summits (the World Bank played a particularly prominent role in the 2002 Monterrey Financing for Development Summit but is also an active participant in virtually all major UN Summits including those on women and environment), the many global meetings on HIV/AIDS (for example the 2006 Toronto International AIDS Summit (16th in the series) and biannual International Conference on AIDS and STIs in Africa (ICASA) meetings in Africa), and a host of other development topics.

The World Bank also plays roles within various aid coordination mechanisms, notably the DAC and OECD.[8] The roles vary from major coordinating efforts on statistics and global monitoring to special efforts to address development topics, like education curriculum reform or procurement systems for purchases of goods and services. Finally, the World Bank participates in special mechanisms like the Paris Club, the informal group led by the French Treasury which negotiates bilateral debt rescheduling and relief arrangements.

Aid harmonization is a sign of creative action and the widespread availability of talent, resources, and ideas for development. Efforts to harmonize the chaotic system are also a symptom of maladies that arise from the complex partnerships and active engagement of myriad actors in the development business today. The World Bank plays different roles in different countries, sometimes central and powerful, sometimes one of many players in arrangements among various governments, UNDP, and other UN agencies. Aid harmonization is very much a work in progress.

Vertical funds

A phenomenon of recent years, at the global and regional levels, has been the birth of a large and proliferating number of programs, coordination mechanisms, and institutions with special mandates for specific development issues. The most prominent example is the Global Fund for AIDS, Tuberculosis and Malaria. The World Bank plays a variety of roles in many if not all of these initiatives, sometimes simply as a partner or observer, more often with specific responsibilities, including in many cases fiduciary roles. A battery of meetings and structures supports efforts to harmonize aid, ranging from specific initiatives that focus on procurement and accounting to, for example, much broader initiatives that aim to mobilize and coordinate aid. An example is the Three One's principle, supported by many agencies in response to the happy but complex proliferation of HIV/AIDS programs. This principle aims to ensure that each nation has one government-led HIV/AIDS program, one national coordination mechanism, and one monitoring and reporting mechanism.

Country and sector aid coordination

Aid coordination mechanisms for individual countries have been in place for several decades in many countries, and they work in different ways with differing effectiveness. These mechanisms fall into three main categories: consultative groups of development partners, which entail periodic meetings co-chaired by a government and the Bank; round-tables, led by the United Nations Development Programme (UNDP), which have similar broad objectives; and aid consortia, which are generally specific to India, Pakistan, and Bangladesh and have a some-what more formal character. In most well-functioning countries, the government also convenes regular meetings of aid partners, which may take elaborate forms based on structured working groups.

The sector lending approach—with the unlikely name of SWAP, for sector-wide approach—also reflects an effort to introduce more order into developing countries. This approach aims to ensure that external financing supports a government-defined and government-led medium-term development program; to ensure a common approach among aid partners and agreed-upon programming; and to coordinate visiting missions, information-gathering efforts, and negotiations on policy and program shifts. SWAPs are becoming the norm in many countries, though they are (by definition) complex and demanding to organize, and rarely if ever operate in an ideal manner. The most common con-cerns are about health programs, because of the large overlap among donors; the most successful are probably in transport which lends itself well to practical coordination.

World Bank partnerships

The issues of coordination and sorting out institutional mandates start within the World Bank itself and its Washington, DC headquarters. The World Bank's history (Chapter 2) explains how several distinct institu-tions came to constitute the World Bank Group. While the International Bank for Reconstruction and Development (IBRD) and the Interna-tional Development Association (IDA) are inextricably integrated for all operational purposes, this is less the case for the other entities.

In practice, the most significant coordination issues arise for IFC. IFC is the largest and most distinctive World Bank affiliate, with its own staff of 2,400 and a separate management, legal department, personnel function, and evaluation mechanism, all housed in a separate building.[9] IFC's finances (it had $14.1 billion in capital in 2007) are also separate from those of the World Bank, as are its operations. IFC prides itself on its dynamism and private-sector, entrepreneurial, can-do culture. Over the years many initiatives have addressed the dual objective of ensuring reasonable harmony between the Bank, with its public sector focus and ethos, and IFC's private sector orientation entrepreneurial spirit, but also ensuring a firewall between the two where conflicts of interest can arise (as they did, for example, in the case of the Argentina financial crisis where IFC investments were severely at risk). Several efforts to merge Bank and IFC departments and programs have met mixed success. Perhaps the best example of successful coordination is the annual *Doing Business* survey and reports,[10] which is widely cited as a practical example both of leadership in identifying bottlenecks to investment and positive harmony among the Bank and IFC.

Box 4.2   Highlights of IFC

The International Finance Corporation's (IFC's) mission is to promote sustainable private-sector development in lower-income countries, with a particular focus on encouraging the growth of productive enterprise and efficient capital markets in member countries. IFC makes loans, takes equity, and provides advisory assistance. It invests in companies and financial institutions in emerging markets, with the broad aim of creating jobs, building economies, and generating tax revenues. IFC is increasingly conscious of its environmental role, and has taken the lead in promoting a widely admired set of investment principles aimed at raising standards of behavior known as the Equator Principles.[11]

IFC works with the International Bank for Reconstruction and Development (IBRD) and International Development Association (IDA) in many parts of the world, on joint operations and strategies. An interesting example is the joint small and medium enterprise development program in Africa.

At the end of June, 2007, IFC's total committed portfolio stood at $25.4 billion. During that fiscal year, its new operations totaled $8.2 billion for 299 projects in 69 countries.

ICSID and MIGA are far smaller institutions, each with quite specialized though important functions; these are briefly summarized in Boxes 4.3 and 4.4. Coordination issues do arise, especially on complex guarantee arrangements like those involved in the Chad Cameroon pipeline but have been successfully addressed on a case-by-case basis.

Box 4.3 ICSID highlights

The International Center for the Settlement of Investment Disputes (ICSID), the smallest institution of the World Bank Group, was created in 1966 partly to relieve the Bank president and staff of burdens arising as they were drawn into a series of complex international disputes. ICSID was to promote international investment by supporting proactive work and mediation in disputes between governments and foreign investors. Established through the Convention on the Settlement of Investment Disputes between States and Nationals of Other States, it consists of an Administrative Council, chaired by the World Bank president, with one representative of each nation that has ratified the convention and a secretariat.

ICSID operates as an autonomous international organization with close links with the World Bank. ICSID expenses are funded out of the Bank's budget, but costs of individual proceedings are borne by the parties involved. Recourse to ICSID conciliation and arbitration is entirely voluntary, but once the parties have consented to arbitration under the ICSID convention, neither can unilaterally withdraw its consent. The convention requires ICSID contracting states—whether or not they are parties to the dispute—to recognize and enforce ICSID arbitral awards. Investment contracts between governments and investors commonly include provisions on ICSID arbitration. Some 20 investment laws and more than 900 bilateral investment treaties also include advance consent by governments to submit investment disputes to ICSID arbitration. Arbitration under the auspices of ICSID is one of the main mechanisms for settling investment disputes under four recent multilateral treaties: the North American Free Trade Agreement, the Energy Charter Treaty, the Cartagena Free Trade Agreement, and the Colonia Investment Protocol of Mercosur. ICSID has seen an increasing flow of cases in recent years.

The World Bank also works closely with several "privileged" partners which have close links to the World Bank though they are autonomous entities, housed under the same roof. The GEF stands out among these separate multi-stakeholder organizations. Established by donor governments in 1991 to provide financing for conservation in connection with the Earth Summit, it funds (through grants) projects and programs that aim to protect the global environment. Projects focus on a wide range of areas, including biodiversity, climate change, international waters, land degradation, the ozone layer, and persistent organic pollutants. GEF is an independent financial organization with a separate staff, but most are World Bank employees. Since 1991, GEF has provided grants for more than 1,300 projects in 140 countries.[12] GEF funds are replenished periodically, most recently in 2006 with $3.13 billion.

Box 4.4   MIGA highlights

The Multilateral Investment Guarantee Agency (MIGA), the newest member of the World Bank Group, began operations in 1988. Like the International Center for the Settlement of Investment Disputes (ICSID), its central purpose is to encourage private investment in developing countries. However, in MIGA's case it insures investors against the risk of transfer restrictions on resources (including inconvertibility of currencies, expropriation of property, war and civil disturbance, and breach of contract). Investors and entities from MIGA member countries—other than the country in which the investment is being made—are eligible for MIGA guarantees, which last from 3 to 15 years, and occasionally 20 years. MIGA focuses on infrastructure development, frontier markets, conflict-affected countries, and South-South investments. The organization consists of a small separate secretariat, but for most intents and purposes is integrated with the World Bank.[13]

The Consultative Group to Assist the Poor (CGAP) focuses on microfinance, and also has special status as an independent organization housed within the World Bank. Formed as a consortium of 33 public and private development agencies, its aim is to expand access to financial services for the poor in developing countries. CGAP's membership structure and global network make it a potent platform for forging consensus on standards and norms for the microfinance industry. With a permanent staff of 35 people and an annual budget of about $10 million, CGAP has become a highly respected resource center on microfinance, providing advisory services, training, research and development, consensus building on standards, and information dissemination.

Partnerships and the development grant facility

Partnership, in a World Bank context, often, though certainly not always, implies a financial relationship, and because in its essence the

World Bank is not organized or basically mandated as an individual grant-making organization, an array of different arrangements have taken shape to allow the Bank to provide at least some funding for innovative, seminal ideas, always with the idea that these grants are catalytic and work strategically toward sustainability. A program known as the Development Grants Facility (DGF) has developed (it was started in 1997) to ensure strategic focus and discipline in what has become a highly complex system. Annual grants under the DGF program in a single year have ranged around $175 million, with some 55 separate partnership arrangements that fall under this rubric. They range from large grants to continuing programs like the Post-Conflict Fund and the CGIAR to very small grants, administered through the small grants programs, generally by country offices.

Under this rubric, the Bank manages several types of funding mechanisms geared to providing grants directly to civil society organizations, with annual block grants for three separate programs. Prominent among these are small grants funds (ranging from $15,000 to $1 million), geared to supporting civil society activities in specific areas such as environment, micro-credit, post-conflict reconstruction, information technology, human rights, gender, and innovative practices as well as activities supporting the aspirations of the indigenous peoples. The Bank also administers, with support from trust funds, several special programs, including prominently the Japan Social Development Fund which is designed to promote innovation through community-based programs. There are also other funds, for example for governance supported by the Dutch government and poverty and social development by the UK. In fiscal 2006, the largest trust funds were the Global Fund for HIV/AIDS, Malaria and Tuberculosis, the GEF and Highly Indebted Poor Country Initiative (HIPC) (59 percent of the total trust funds administered by the Bank of $10.29 billion).

Several independent organizations that work closely with the World Bank in fact began as units within the Bank itself (often with trust fund and/or DGF funding) and later became independent. Several are referred to as spin-offs, though each has a quite distinct history and institutional form. The Development Gateway Foundation illustrates the phenomenon of a Bank spin-off organization. Launched with the passionate support of James Wolfensohn to capture the potential of information technology to support development, it is today an international nonprofit that provides Web-based platforms to make aid programs more effective. The foundation aims to improve aid management and coordination and government procurement by providing more information and enhancing transparency; leverage the Internet to bolster communication among development practitioners worldwide; and help build country information systems. DGF runs AiDA (Accessible Information on Development Activities), a large online directory that offers a quick overview of who is doing what in international development, where they are doing it, and with what funds. AiDA lists some 130,000 ongoing or planned activities worldwide, plus 400,000 archived projects and programs. Information comes from major bilateral donors, multilateral development banks, and UN agencies.[14]

World Links is a second spin-off. Now an independent not-for-profit enterprise, it also works with information technology as its main instrument—in this case linking children and classrooms to bring opportunity and hope to disadvantaged youth across the world. By offering training and access to computers and the Internet, World Links aims to enhance the skills, knowledge, attitudes, and insight of youth to enable them to participate in the local and global economy.[15]

Many more such institutions and entities sit within or are affiliated with the World Bank, including institutions as widely different as the GDN (with its ambitious agenda of encouraging development research) and the World Faiths Development Dialogue (WFDD).[16] This latter was created to foster active dialogue among faith institutions, who were engaged in development issues but often critical of the World Bank, and development institutions. Controversy around its creation and mandate in 2000 highlighted the tensions that have emerged (see Chapter 6) both on the proper reach of the World Bank's mandate and the benefits and disadvantages of the spin-off arrangements which can both assure independent focus on specific issues but also run the risk of exacerbating coordination issues.

Two partnership programs run by the World Bank merit special mention, given their important historic role and continuing significance. The CGIAR is a strategic alliance among countries, regional and international organizations, and private foundations that support 15 international agricultural centers. The science that made possible the Green Revolution of the 1960s and 1970s (by developing and introducing what were considered "miracle" crops for maize, rice and wheat, inter alia) was largely the work of CGIAR centers and their national agricultural research partners. Today CGIAR centers work with national partners, civil society groups, and the private sector to respond to emerging development challenges and generate public goods available to all. CGIAR's more recent achievements include varieties of high-protein maize released in 25 countries, new rices that are transforming agriculture in West Africa, and a strain of tilapia that shows a 70 percent gain in growth rate. CGIAR has operated since 1971, and more than 8,500 CGIAR scientists and staff now work in more than 100 countries.[17]

Working within the World Bank since 1987 under a special financing agreement with the Japanese government is the World Bank Graduate Scholarship Program. Each year the program awards scholarships to individuals from Bank member countries to study subjects related to economic development at renowned universities. The program has awarded some 3,500 scholarships to students selected from among nearly 53,000 applicants, supported by more than $174.1 million from the government of Japan. The program aims to help create an international community of highly trained professionals working in economic and social development, to support people committed to public service in their countries, and to offer the opportunity to dedicated civil servants (only people with work experience and who have not previously studied abroad are eligible). The World Bank and the government of Japan require the scholars to return to their home countries.

An exercise that combines the finest aspects of the World Bank's development thinking with some of its pitfalls in the development marketplace. The idea is inspirational: to bring together a host of ideas in a free-wheeling marketplace where proposals, small and large, from all directions and institutions, are aired and have the chance to attract both attention and, in a competitive process, some finance. The program is funded from the DGF. Held annually at the World Bank headquarters, a feast of ideas come together with at least some of the booths that house individual projects pointing the way towards new trends and challenges to conventional wisdom. The model has proved so popular that World Bank country offices in many countries hold local development marketplace events. Various foundations and others support the work.

Some proposals are outstanding and projects supported through the marketplace have been the source of important initiatives. Overall, however, it is questionable whether an annual competitive event can do much more than symbolize the array of ideas that exists in the entrepreneurial world of development practitioners. Finding better ways to support good ideas and flexible partnerships, most falling outside formal government programs, deserves careful reflection.

Partnerships with IFIs

The World Bank has special relationships with a wide range of financial institutions that are not formally affiliated with the Bank Group.

The most significant and, in many respects the most complex, is with the IMF which, though it sits directly across the street from the World Bank headquarters and shares many governance features (including an almost identical weighted voting structure) operates with very different procedures and organizational culture. Issues of coordination are outlined in Chapter 2, insofar as they were an integral part of the two institutions' histories, through the debt and oil crises, the East Asia financial crisis, and other financial crises. The effort to bring the two into closer working harmony is a continuing effort and challenge.

Other prominent partners are the regional development banks— sometimes termed the multilateral development banks, or MDBs. When the system works smoothly, the World Bank and its regional bank counterparts actively cooperate, as they did during the Asian financial crisis of 1997–9. When such crises occur, the respective parties work out a pragmatic division of responsibilities, taking the lead in arenas where they have the capacity and special interest to do so. History also includes instances of rivalry and discord, however, and successive efforts to harmonize policies and approaches between the Bank and the MDB family are common. A general rule of thumb is that the regional banks are more oriented in governance structure and ethos to the region in question than the World Bank. A Global Institutions book by Jonathan Strand addresses this important group of institutions in greater detail.

The regional banks were each established independently, though their overall structures generally resemble the World Bank's. At a simplistic level they are sometimes described as "regional clones," though in practice each has a quite distinct structure, financing base, and ethos. The first such institution was the Inter-American Development Bank (IADB), established in 1959, but the product of protracted discussions tracing back to 1890. Based in Washington, DC, IADB is an active player across Latin America on a wide range of issues. The African Development Bank (AfDB), which has special ties to the Organization for African Unity, was founded in 1964, and began operations in 1966. Like the World Bank Group, AfDB has hard and soft lending windows (that is, its lending includes market terms like IBRD and concessional terms like those of IDA). It was caught in the turmoil facing Africa in the 1990s particularly its debt woes, but today is solidly established and operating from Tunis. The Asian Development Bank (ADB), which has had particularly close ties to Japan, was established in 1966, and the European Bank for Reconstruction and Development (EBRD) followed in 1991, as part of the international response to the transition in Eastern Europe and the former Soviet

Union. EBRD stands out for its explicit focus on encouraging a transition to democracy, and thus has a notably more forthright approach to its political role than the World Bank.

A wide array of other institutions also work closely with the World Bank, many under special partnership arrangements. Prominent among these are the International Fund for Agricultural Development (IFAD), established after the first oil shocks to redirect surplus oil revenues toward development. Other prominent partners include the Islamic Development Bank, the Nordic Development Bank, and the OPEC Fund for International Development (OPEC Fund). Subregional banks—classified as multilateral banks although they are owned by a group of countries—also play important roles. These include the Corporación Andina de Fomento (CAF), the Caribbean Development Bank (CDB), the Central American Bank for Economic Integration (CABEI), East African Development Bank (EADB), and the West African Development Bank (BOAD). Last but certainly not least are close and complex relationships with the European Commission which is deeply involved in development; the European Investment Bank (EIB) is an important partner.

The World Bank and its bully pulpit

A final comment concerns what is sometimes termed the World Bank's bully pulpit: that is, the opportunity to preach (in a positive sense) on the need to mobilize support for aid in general and good development ideas in particular. The Bank's privileged place does give it unique opportunities to play this role, and a special obligation to use it well. This calls for both careful analysis of facts and wisdom in discerning the most effective approaches to development, for communicating well and fairly, and for ensuring balance among differing viewpoints. The ethical challenges involved in this role are enormous, if too rarely recognized by the World Bank today.

The challenges involve tensions among the wish to present a continuing powerful voice of advocacy for both poverty initiatives and foreign aid and the genuine complexity of the issues and discordant voices, even within the World Bank, about the best path for development. The World Bank as a respected and rigorous analyst of development issues has earned a place in many leading global forums, notable among them the G8 group of global leaders. The World Bank's annual meetings are a major focal point for debates about development and its reports are looked to as pivotal sources of information, ideas, and guidance on priorities. As a prominent example,

Bill Gates attributes the first step in his remarkable focus on global health issues to inspiration and insight gained from reading the World Bank's World Development Report (WDR) on health, over and over again.[18] The World Bank's advocacy for the cause of development in the Doha round of trade discussions, with analytic work linked to advocacy with moral overtones, is another example. This is all to the good. The issues arise when the World Bank, in its fervor to promote the cause of development, strays too far in stating the case for specific action without recognizing the drawbacks and viewpoints of others, or when its research agenda is shaped by its vision of the outcome it seeks. To retain the respect and to be the credible, passionate but truthful advocate it seeks to be, the World Bank needs to keep always in mind a sense of humility that appreciates the enormous complexity of the task, respects the roles of many other actors involved in development, and is always willing to look to new evidence and ideas and change its positions when appropriate.

Another challenge for all development partners is to ensure that the time devoted to tending partnerships is not at a superficial level, and that the partnerships are always aimed at ensuring that development results are made more efficient, effective, and more powerfully seen and felt by client countries.

Summary

The World Bank is an integral part of the elaborate and dynamic international development arrangements that are sometimes loosely called the aid community. It has been a leader in global efforts, propelled forward especially after the Millennium and Monterrey UN Summits, to mobilize large additional amounts of aid to fight poverty and to ensure that it is well and harmoniously used. Here, it works with the OECD and DAC and several bilateral and multilateral partners. It also engages with the G8 and major global and regional entities. Ongoing aid harmonization processes aim to address the many dysfunctional aspects of aid arrangements that involve many very different organizations, with overlap and uncoordinated objectives, approaches, and procedures.

The Bank continues its long history of working to help governments coordinate aid at the country level, with important mechanisms being the consultative group and, more recently, an increasing focus on coordinated sector based operations (SWAPs).The Bank has multiple and quite complex working relationships with many UN agencies, the most prominent being the UNDP since the Bank and UNDP share formal coordination responsibilities at both global and country level for aid partnership arrangements.

The Bank works closely with other IFIs, notably the IMF and the regional development banks and export credit agencies. It faces significant challenges in coordinating partnerships even within the World Bank Group (notably with the IFC, its private sector arm) but also with the wide array of affiliated organizations, large and small, including some that are integral parts of the organization and others that are spun off. Civil society organizations, private companies and foundations are also part of the complex tapestry of aid coordination challenges.

5 Grounding in realities
The World Bank at work

The preceding narrative, reviewing the World Bank's history and operational nuts and bolts, can make for rather dry reading, but the institution's day-to-day work is replete with fascinating events, complex issues, and choices. This chapter presents 16 short examples that illustrate facets of the Bank's work, the roles it plays, and the dilemmas and constraints it faces on the ground. What does a project look like and how does it differ from a sector operation and an adjustment loan? How do relationships with country officials work? How does the Bank really work with civil society? How does the Bank's intellectual work relate to its financing? What does the Bank do when it suspects corrupt practices? How does the Bank change and from what impetus? What are the boundaries of its reach and action?

Drawn from the author's direct experience, the narratives are not fully inclusive of all regions and sectors, but they cover major areas of World Bank operations and partnerships (lending for projects, sectors, and policy; analytic work; aid coordination; and country relationships). They thus exemplify the diversity and complexity of development challenges, the pragmatic nature of the Bank's approaches and actions, and the real opportunities and limitations as to what it can achieve in its partner role. Each vignette tells a fragment of the story, and concludes with some questions and some "morals" it suggests. There are thousands of stories like these—most go unwritten; the subject is a veritable gold mine for future research.

Project lending: learning from cattle ranching in Madagascar

Madagascar's midwestern region (around the town of Tsiroanmandidy)—its rolling grasslands sparsely peopled—was ideal, it seemed to visiting livestock experts, for a truly modern ranching operation, modeled on a blend of Australian and Texan techniques. Such a project would help modernize Madagascar's traditional cattle industry and bring rich returns. The Malagasy government negotiators, both technical and financial, also seemed enthusiastic and agreed willingly to a long series of detailed proposals, signing a loan agreement with the World Bank in 1968.

The project was plagued with problems from the beginning. The (all foreign) technical assistance team spoke no French, could find no horses to ride, and was surprised to find that imported Brahman bulls lost weight and then died one by one. French livestock specialists at a nearby research station watched the operation with some contempt, as the planning process had largely ignored their long-standing knowledge, largely because of cultural miscommunication. Villagers were so hostile to the ranching scheme that grassfires they set were a constant problem. Then cattle thieves got to work. They operated so blatantly that they would round up cattle, slaughter them on the spot, and leave the ears on the barbed wire fences. The ranching team (a group of experts hired and largely supervised by the World Bank) dimly perceived that major political change was in the air, but hardly realized its repercussions for the project. In fact, a new government was embarking on revolutionary changes that involved many U-turns in policy, including a new recognition of traditional land tenure rights of villagers, which previously were simply ignored. Tensions between the Malagasy and French governments (the latter the former colonial power which had hitherto exercised wide influence in Madagascar), resulted in upheavals throughout the government, economy and society.

The changing situation doomed a project which was already faltering to failure, at virtually every level (social, technical, financial, institutional). Though there was little question that, technically, ranching could have succeeded if it had meshed with the sociopolitical situation, in that tumultuous climate there was little hope for success. The foreign advisor team could engage no one in the government to figure out what to do, so the diminished ranchers fumed and struggled on in lonely isolation.

Under these unpromising circumstances, a second project was prepared that reflected important lessons from the first and looked in much more sensible directions, to a village-based livestock development scheme farther west. It involved some, albeit cursory, effort to engage the local communities in planning. That project, approved in 1974, however, also faced many struggles, partly because Madagascar's political situation remained tenuous, but also because communities were not genuinely engaged in planning and managing the scheme. Economic policies on pricing (which fixed meat prices well below their market levels to benefit urban consumers) undercut incentives to producers to change their practices.

The sad reality is that the promise of developing a livestock industry in Madagascar suffered severe blows during the nation's long political transition which are felt to this day, and successive project schemes were simply unable to overcome the large obstacles. The Bank's support has evolved from the almost stylized project approach of the first ranching project, to efforts to engage communities, to much more focus on policy instruments and financial and managerial issues at the level of the livestock and, more broadly, the agricultural sector.

The experience illustrates well the severe limits on area-specific, project-based approaches, and the growing appreciation for the vital role which broad sector institutions and policies play down to the community level. The Bank's broadening approach from narrow project approaches to a sector-wide focus and lending instruments, and major efforts to link project and macroeconomic experience reflect the kind of project failure experienced in the Madagascar case. The Bank's blinders or self-imposed restrictions on addressing political factors also are illustrated by this story, a tale repeated in many situations across Africa during the difficult decades of the 1970s and 1980s.

Other, somewhat more obvious lessons learned from such experience were the importance of using sociological knowledge, that local people must be truly engaged if schemes are to work, and that unadapted "recipes" for change from other parts of the world will not work. Weak links, within the World Bank, between macroeconomic analysis and advice and project experience on the ground—problems that were then fairly characteristic of the World Bank—delayed an understanding of what was happening on both fronts.

Adjustment and social crisis in Bolivia

In a situation of apocalyptic economic catastrophe—with inflation running at around 25,000 percent a year—a new government took office in Bolivia in 1985, determined on radical economic reform. The convictions of this government about what they needed to do were so clear that officials drafted their proposals as laws, not plans, and their actions went beyond what many outside advisors had dared to suggest. They took step after step in what constituted true shock therapy, including large devaluations of the currency, closing the money-losing mining company, intervening banks, and sharply reducing tariffs. As the remedies began to take effect, new possibilities for relationships with development partners (which had been largely somnolent through the crisis) opened up.

The World Bank had played a frustrated but thoughtful role during the years of economic turmoil, struggling to solve the insolvable problems of several floundering projects, but above all presenting a probing report that analyzed the economic situation facing the country and laid out at least some options. Now (as the government reform program kicked into gear) a decision was made to move into a bold action mode—to remove all stops to allow the promising reforms to succeed. The World Bank created a brand-new unit and engaged a new team to pursue these changes, and gave it license and resources. The rough plan of action was that the World Bank would provide fast-disbursing resources first to finance urgent imports that would jump-start the economy, followed by structural adjustment credits that would support broader economic reforms; would relaunch an aid coordination group (there was a carcass of a Bolivia Consultative Group from years before), so that Bolivia's case for financing would find a ready hearing in the international community; would undertake a rich menu of new studies of key areas, including agriculture and export prospects; and would quickly prepare a series of new projects supporting inter alia urban management and financial controls (which were in dismal shape). The International Monetary Fund (IMF) was to play an important role, and put what was then a brand-new World Bank/IMF instrument—the Policy Framework Paper (PFP)—on an accelerated course, in hopes that it would persuade the entire aid community to address what was understood to be an impossible debt situation and justify higher financing, especially from the International Development Association (IDA).

While frictions sometimes occurred among the development partners, and between them and government officials, this was a heady time full of energy and hope. The partnership was in important respects exemplary, as it was grounded in mutual respect and a fairly clear idea of comparative advantage among the participating agencies. There was no question about who was in the driver's seat: the Bolivian government. The most complex relationships involved the IMF, and they crystallized around how far the PFP could and should serve as a strategic document or help ground a more technical IMF program (a prerequisite then and now for many kinds of international finance). Various high-powered personalities interacted in reasonably good spirits, among them Jeffrey Sachs, advisor to the Bolivian government, and Gonzalo Sanchez de Losada, then planning minister and later

Bolivia's president. A high point for the partnership was a weeklong strategy brainstorming session in the Yungas region that brought together senior government leaders from various sectors, opposition leaders, and key development partners. This freewheeling discussion of issues and options symbolized a dynamic partnership and it produced decisions and changes in course.

Everyone involved in the early planning days had barely considered one topic: the social implications of needed but drastic economic reforms. Participants understood, with regret, that Bolivia's education and health sectors, however needy, were largely untouchable; the sectors were in shambles and, while Bolivia's future depended on them, the political situation was such that even courageous leaders were hesitant to move in significant ways. Teachers' unions were dominated by Trotskyites, for example, and they mobilized often violent demonstrations at even a whiff of reform. Thus these vital issues were postponed by the government for better times (in retrospect a harder fight should have been fought by all concerned). More immediate issues came to dominate the picture. As the shambolic parastatal tin mining company, Corporación Minera de Bolivia (COMIBOL) was drastically downsized, opposition from Bolivia's civil society began to mount, especially from miners who were out of work. The decisions to reform and privatize COMIBOL were an essential element in the program to reform the economy, and few doubted the need for radical surgery, as the cost of producing tin in Bolivia exceeded any likely earnings, but the fate of thousands of miners and their families was left largely to the very feeble market. The miners marched on La Paz, and some violent incidents ensued. New ideas were needed.

The World Bank had no ready recipe for such circumstances, so the team searched widely for inspiration. Sensing the urgency, Jeffrey Sachs, as a leading economic advisor, urged a transfusion of funds for social works. Other voices (including some in the Bank and their academic advisors) cautioned that this was a recipe for disaster, given weak management capacity and rampant corruption. Meetings with a hastily assembled brain trust, discussions in Bolivia, and consultations with other aid agencies encouraged the World Bank team to respond quickly to a proposal from the Bolivian government to create an Emergency Social Fund that would support a raft of small projects presented by communities and nongovernmental organizations (NGOs). The government wanted the Bank to respond in days, sensing the urgency, while the normal gestation period for a Bank-financed project was a minimum of nine months. Further, the World Bank was entering one of its more turbulent internal periods, as it was about to launch a shadowy but far-reaching reorganization, essentially paralyzing most decisions. But a combination of good fortune, determination—including mobilizing energetic younger staff members and securing the blessing of the rumored new vice president for Latin America—and the decision-making vacuum allowed the Bank team to engage with leading government officials on a fleshed out design for the program (incorporating, for example, measures to assure full transparency, with quarterly publication of financial accounts), and to secure approval for the pilot project by the World Bank board (with IDA financing) at record speed. The performance of the Bolivian team that launched the emergency social fund (ESF) justified the leap of faith, and again with unprecedented speed—though this time with far more questioning within the World Bank, and insistence on impossible-to-achieve precision in targets for planning and monitoring—IDA approved a second credit (an interest-free loan—see Chapter 3) only six months later.

The ESF came nowhere near solving Bolivia's social problems and tensions, but it had the positive result of focusing far more attention on them and, by supporting a wide range of community initiatives, brought real benefits to thousands of people. It did not end poverty— systems for reaching the poorest Bolivians were simply not there. But it was an important first step. And the program had many obstacles to navigate, not least of them ferocious political pressures in Bolivia to direct funding to "desirable" corners. Avoiding politics was an early concern of the ESF team and remained at the fore; political considerations inevitably crept into decision-making, but the location of the ESF in the office of Bolivia's president and its autonomy allowed the teams to avoid many pressures. The design of the ESF included a sunset clause for ending operations, because the teams (Bolivian and World Bank) understood that political pressures would mount with time.

The ESF was remarkably successful in supporting a wide range of excellent programs that benefited many people, especially in the cities. It was run with a dynamism and openness that helped turn the tide of negative perceptions about the drastic economic reforms that were underway—in Bolivia and within the international community. An unanticipated outcome was that the experience opened the door to a new form of social fund lending for the World Bank, essentially programs explicitly channeling support to small community-based projects to address immediate needs and test new avenues to local development. Social funds in many forms have since benefited communities in all corners of the world. In several cases, Bolivian ESF veterans have helped advise planners on designing such funds in places as far away as Cambodia.

The Bolivia story illustrates a positive case of country-driven reforms which the World Bank, the IMF, and other donors supported with vigor. Many of the unfortunate aspects of such crisis-driven reforms, especially their failure to take sufficient account of social repercussions, played out in Bolivia but the gaps in reform programs were recognized quite quickly and swift action was taken to respond through the new, though untested instrument of the ESF. The ESF worked remarkably well because of its strong Bolivian leaders and served as a best practice model across many countries in ensuing years. The Bank was able to play a central and constructive role throughout, through a program that was able to link analysis with lending with timely advice and support in aid mobilization.

Strategic options for Bolivia

Articulating a strategic vision for Bolivia's future was not easy during the turbulent period of economic reform in 1985–7. Mining and natural gas had provided most export revenues, but mining prospects were dismal, and a multiyear contract to export natural gas to Argentina was running out, with little prospect of renewal. Exporting gas to Brazil was a prospect but clearly many years off. Agriculture was in deep trouble, and industrial enterprises fared even worse. Some form of credible vision was urgently needed. This was true, obviously, for Bolivia's political leaders, but the development partners also needed a promising path if they were to work the miracle of changing multiple rules about buying back and rescheduling some of Bolivia's debt, to engage in new kinds of projects, and justify the levels of concessional finance that the country needed.

As part of its work, the World Bank Bolivia team invited several rather unconventional experts to explore options. One was an iconoclastic economist on the verge of dropping his economic career to study psychology (David Morawetz), the other a British politician with a passionate interest in development and creative private-sector partnerships (Colin Moynihan). Moynihan spurred thinking about responses to social needs and was able to convey, from his perspective as a skilled politician, that the World Bank needed to communicate in far more meaningful ways (i.e., not bureaucratic) about development. He also pressed successfully with some receptive World Bank leaders to make addressing the economic and social impact of the coca industry and drug policies a central goal (a first for the Bank and one that left many mightily uneasy).

Morawetz traveled to all corners of Bolivia with a mandate to address the question: what next? In the process he visited the Santa

Cruz region in Bolivia's vast eastern lowland region and met a visionary man with a plan. The plan was bold: to use the Parana River as the Mississippi of South America, carrying exports of soybeans and other crops, and opening doors to new settlement in a region that offered more promise than the harsh environment of Bolivia's Altiplano. This vision was the heart of Morawetz's report, which the Consultative Group discussed at its 1988 meeting. The report served many purposes, including encouraging studies of projects in eastern Bolivia, but above all it helped turn the pessimism of the time by illustrating promising and plausible prospects.

Despite this promise, the Bank's later narratives about this period told a pessimistic story of the eastern plains. An eastern lowlands program was indeed approved, but heavily weighted toward planning and environmental studies rather than concrete projects. The program was not completed, and there is little evidence that any actors ever took the expensive and voluminous environmental studies seriously into account. The World Bank's official narratives of its role in Bolivia were entirely silent about the strategic reviews undertaken at a critical juncture to help define options and new paths. There was no mention of any role the Bank might have played in shifting the center of gravity from Bolivia's highlands toward the lowlands. Nervousness about environmental critics (who were uneasy about development in the lowlands region) played a part, but a new World Bank team with different priorities was chronicling events and they looked to the present, not the past.

Yet the story has a fascinating sequel. Morawetz revisited Bolivia in 2004 and was stunned by positive changes in the Santa Cruz region. Soybean and other production had expanded rapidly, private companies like Del Monte, the food giant, were investing, the area's population was growing, and the overall ambience was dynamic and hopeful. The World Bank agricultural project must, he suggested, have produced one of the highest returns on record.

This unusual story suggests important lessons about the Bank's work and roles. The advice given, much of it informal and unofficial, played roles arguably as important as finance and formal analysis. In times of crisis, especially, this kind of advice is critically important. Further, the elusive element of hope and plausible strategic vision proved to be as important for turning Bolivia's prospects as detailed plans and concrete investments. The combination of a healthy and confident partnership between the World Bank and the Bolivian government, and the fortuitous circumstance of a leadership vacuum inside the Bank that opened special possibilities for creative options (considering the coca issue frontally and undertaking the informal strategic explorations), made possible much broader thinking than was the norm. Its payoff was handsome despite its limited renown.

Partnership challenges: confronting tense relationships in Senegal

Relationships between the World Bank team and the government of Senegal in 1997 were cordial on the surface but beneath lay many tensions. The precipitating issue was World Bank reluctance to continue a series of fast-disbursing IDA credits supporting the government's structural adjustment program and even to release part of an already approved credit because, in its view, the government had failed to deliver on its promises. The government, in its turn, badly and urgently wanted the credits to help address yawning gaps in the government budget. The Bank's reluctance arose from what it viewed as disappointing performance, which it saw as reflecting limited government commitment to reforms that had been discussed and agreed upon in painstaking detail. The government was frustrated that a Bank team (which included several new faces) seemed not to understand the country's needs and unique qualities. The French government was encouraging the Bank to move ahead with releasing funds, but its in-depth knowledge of Senegal's deep-seated structural problems tempered the pressure it was willing to exert on the Bank to speed up lending.

During a rather formal, somewhat tense meeting with Senegal's president, the World Bank's country director suggested that a broad and open airing of issues might help the relationship chart a new path, and, though such a process was not in the script, the president responded warmly. He instructed his finance minister to pursue the idea, and in early 1999 an ambitious meeting in Sale, near Dakar, occurred over several days. It included the full leadership team from the World Bank's Sahel Department, much of the economic cabinet of Senegal, the leader of the opposition (Abdoulaye Wade, now Senegal's president), and key members of the development community.

The meeting was called Journées de Reflection—Days of Reflection—and it began in the rather formal style that was the norm in relationships between the Bank and external partners. However, sparks soon began to fly as the World Bank team bluntly put its assessment of Senegal's deep problems on the table. The government countered with criticisms of the Bank, and a stark difference in views became evident as never before: the World Bank team compared

Senegal's situation to the Great Depression, while the government portrayed it as one requiring minor tweaking, and above all predictable and large-scale external financing. However, despite the apparent rift, a new understanding was born, grounded in the respect that came from honesty and genuine concern. Many of the younger Senegalese present took to heart the challenge and came forward with proposals for study and action that ultimately led to creative and practical programs. The World Bank was able to discuss previously untouchable topics, including the economic impact of the exchange rate for the CFA—the common West African currency, the desperate need for university reform, and poor nutrition of Senegal's poor.

The Journées de Reflection were not and could not be formally programmed, but the willingness of both Senegalese and World Bank leaders to seize on a window of opportunity proved a turning point. Putting the entire program and relationship on the table was high risk, but the gains were also substantial. The story illustrates the kinds of complex pressures that have often been part of structural adjustment discussions and the nuances in partnerships that involved, in this case, Senegal's main international support and former colonial ruler.

Planning for tempest: the CFA devaluation in West Africa

Part of the frustration in dealing with Senegal's problems was that the government could not in fact address the central issue, which was major misalignment of the CFA franc (a common currency tied to the French franc at the time) with price movements in West Africa. The exchange rate between the CFA and the French franc was at the core of relationships with France—its stability not only a matter of pride but also seen as a strategic economic pillar. The CFA had never been devalued since the common currency was created soon after World War II. As it progressively became evident that in time devaluation could not be avoided, it was obvious that change would require an extraordinary decision-making process, with France at its highest government levels in the lead, and the heads of state of 14 African countries (the CFA franc zone members) needing to act in concert. The planning process needed to happen in a disciplined atmosphere of secrecy because if information leaked out the consequences would be serious all around, yet the devaluation would need a major program of support to contend with the economic and social disruptions, involving all 14 countries of the franc zone at the same time. The challenge was immense, not least because it could barely be discussed outside a small inner circle even at the World Bank. One Bank manager who wrote about the need to devalue the CFA came close to losing his job, which had a dampening effect.

The unfolding of the CFA devaluation and the supporting programs in 1993–4 are stories only partially told to date, but are too lengthy to recount here.[1] One feature, however, was particularly worrisome as the moment for decision approached. It was apparent that several of the African heads of state had little appreciation for what a devaluation involved—not surprisingly, since they had never lived through one—and needed informed advice. The World Bank team offered to provide special briefings and set a high standard, offering as professional a briefing as the presidents of the United States or France would demand. Armed with the leading technologies of the time, the Bank's Jean-Louis Sarbib and colleagues presented a complex and dynamic picture of the normal course of devaluations, the reasons why one was essential in this case, the likely social and political repercussions, and the best-practice ideas of the time on how to respond. The top-secret briefings were deeply appreciated and the active discussions, despite being restricted to a small inner circle, were a material influence in planning for the post-devaluation period.

The secret briefings were known only to a few people even within the World Bank, and are not part of the narrative record of its role. The opportunity for such intensive interaction with heads of state does not arise often. In this case, the Bank was able to fill an important need that other partners, because of their relationships and roles, could not. Looking back, that contribution made a difference. More broadly, the Bank's complex role in one of the most complex structural adjustment efforts ever (because of its multi-country character, the great post-adjustment social and economic needs, and the special requirements for secrecy) was demanding on many dimensions, not least the requirements for communication skills and political savvy.

The corruption conundrum in Indonesia

In the summer of 1998, the World Bank team responsible for Indonesia faced challenges on many fronts. The contagion of the East Asia economic and social crisis had spread to Indonesia despite hopes that it would be spared, political change was in the air, huge financing needs had to be addressed, and the future path was far from certain. On top of this, a series of articles in the press suggested not only that corruption was widespread and a major cause of Indonesia's economic and political problems, but also that the World Bank was responsible to a significant extent because it had failed to act despite knowing the problems well. The crisis atmosphere lent urgency to planning, even while it was clear that the situation was taking the Bank in new directions.

It was a *Wall Street Journal* article that raised the greatest concerns. It argued that the World Bank was well aware that corruption was the norm for projects in Indonesia, with "leakage" of as much as 30 percent stemming from pervasive fixing of procurement, cooking of financial statements, and topping up of government salaries with project funds. Further, the article reported a few accusations of corrupt practices on the part of the World Bank staff itself. The Bank's failure to report honestly on corruption in its economic documents and public pronouncements was seen as failing the international community. The article even went on to suggest that an institution that was not forthright in addressing corruption could not be trusted to provide honest data and information.

The litany of accusations was met with shock, because it confronted World Bank staff members about aspects of their work in which they took great pride—above all the rigor and integrity of their economic analyses. Staff members had known about and discussed the corruption issue, but addressing it was not at the top of the priority list, and it was understood to be a subject best addressed in private and over a long time frame as government institutions developed the capacity to manage well. Indignation about the personal accusations against Bank staff also fueled the reaction.

Yet the public debate about corruption in Indonesia also touched responsive chords, and deep-seated concerns among many staff encouraged the Bank to respond. The question was what to do in the face of the uncertain and highly complex economic and political situation in Indonesia and the large scope of the problem. The decision was to field two teams—one aimed at advising the government on possible strategies to address corruption, the second evaluating World Bank policies and practices more specifically.

The reports of the two teams were widely publicized and discussed. It was apparent to both that quick fixes were impossible, and that real action would need to await less turbulent political times, specifically the transition to a new Indonesian government that was then in the offing. Yet both internal and external pressures for visible and immediate action were substantial, however unrealistic.

This crisis-driven exploration of the full range of corruption challenges is part of the story of how issues of governance and corruption produced important changes in the World Bank's thinking, culture and policies. What emerged over time in Indonesia was a creative and dynamic multi-partner consortium addressing governance issues, and a far-reaching soul-searching within the Bank about its implicit over-all approach (seeing corruption too much as oil for the motor, and too little as sand in the engine). Discussions of corruption have never been the same since.

A different corruption story: missing nuts in the Gambia

Concerns about corruption are not new, and the World Bank has been aware of how corruption works and its damaging impact for many years. A relatively small incident in the Gambia in 1992 illustrates how specific issues could arise and what the World Bank tried to do about them.

The Gambia was touted by the IMF and World Bank in the 1990s as a leading economic reformer because it followed many best practice policies of the time, but despite progress, results seemed less than expected, given firm policy action supported by extraordinarily high flows of external financing that supported the government budget and investment projects. The causes of the performance gap could be dis-cerned, in pieces, from successive reports of World Bank project teams, which recounted poor management performance in agency after agency and a pattern of questionable practices such as very fre-quent travel by government teams (who received high per diem allow-ances when they were on the road).

During meetings when implementation issues were the central agenda, an uneasy member of a Bank-financed technical assistance team reported in confidence to a Bank official, that there was a major gap in the finances of the state-run peanut (groundnut) enterprise— essentially, that payments were made for peanuts that were never sup-plied. The Bank did not directly fund the groundnut parastatal but its financing of the overall macroeconomic program gave it a legitimate voice in management issues for an important public sector entity. The amounts missing were substantial: a measurable share of government revenues. The Bank team, which was in Banjul, Gambia's capital, acted swiftly, encouraging the finance minister to agree to an immedi-ate special audit, which confirmed the problem. Those involved were removed from their jobs, though legal prosecution was so slow that it never was concluded.

The case of the missing nuts was relatively minor in itself, if worry-ing, but the discussions opened the door to an unusually forthright discussion of corruption issues involving Gambia's president and other aid partners. These, in turn, led to special project measures to improve parastatal management and address corrupt practices, and also to a weeklong meeting to discuss the relationships between Gambian officials and their development partners that had allowed corrupt practices to develop and persist. The lesson that sharp increases in development financing require special vigilance was well learned, and the subtle tensions between World Bank officials (who tended to suspect many government partners) and government officials (who resented the patronizing and demanding behavior of Bank teams) were openly discussed and thus tempered. The new opening that emerged was sadly brought to an abrupt halt by a military coup d'etat in July 1994.[2]

Diversity in policy perspectives and options: the ASEM trust fund

The East Asian economic crisis of 1997–9 resulted in an extraordinary international mobilization because of its scale, fast pace, and threatened global contagion. Economies that seemed prosperous suddenly faced threats from banking collapse and there were no social safety nets in place to help the millions who lost jobs and faced steep food and medicine price increases. Among the many programs launched with urgency was a new trust fund (with $40 million initially) provided by European nations following a heads-of-state meeting known as ASEM (Asia Europe Meeting) in April 1998 to support post-crisis economic and social reforms. In the overall financing scheme the ASEM fund was a tiny part but it offered important support for the "softer" or the more human dimensions of the reforms that were being implemented at the time.

The European governments asked the World Bank to manage the trust fund, to ensure that it dovetailed with Bank-led financial and technical support for reform, and because speed and efficiency were seen as essential (and they were hopeful that the Bank could deliver on both fronts). The World Bank put much effort into overseeing the trust fund, both because it offered a chance to mobilize much-needed grants in critical arenas such as banking reform and monitoring of social welfare, and because the European interest was obviously important as they were key World Bank members and partners. The trust fund was implemented in an excellent manner, and had the unusual, very useful, and rather unpopular (with country leaders— because it was time-consuming and demanding) requirement that all programs be explicitly set within the context of the World Bank's existing development strategies in the region: how would they fit, and how would good coordination be assured?[3]

The ASEM trust fund, like most development programs, was launched with multiple objectives, the leading one clearly being to support countries at a time of deep need. However, a less-articulated but no less real objective was to balance what was seen as an unduly Anglo-Saxon tenor in outside development advice to East Asian countries, coming from the IMF and World Bank and the US and Australian governments. In considering both financial reforms and the future direction of social policy, the ASEM leaders believed that the European economic and social experience (including its social welfare policies) had been neglected and could prove useful. The authors of the trust fund made clear their intent, but did not tie use of the fund specifically to procurement in Europe, because they understood the need for flexibility. However, their unease grew as trust fund approvals saw successive programs and projects involving a preponderance of Anglo-Saxon and especially US companies and individuals.

The World Bank made efforts on several levels to assure affirmative consideration of European consultants, but those met only part of the need. A more effective response was a special project aimed explicitly at exploring European experience with social policy as it might apply to post-crisis Asia. A series of commissioned papers and eight conferences proved the merits of the hypothesis that European experience was a valuable and rather neglected field of exploration, and that an active effort to mine that experience was feasible and worthwhile.[4]

Experience with the ASEM trust fund illustrates the significant advantages of such trust funds, which have become an important part of World Bank operations. Each one arises from different historical circumstances and has its own arrangements. However in general, trust funds can complement World Bank operations, and make it possible to do what could not be done with existing Bank resources. The dual challenge of keeping the focus on core objectives, and ensuring that the Bank, when it assumes responsibility for a trust fund, devotes sufficient resources to the effort, were well illustrated here, with largely positive results. The story also illustrates how multiple objectives for aid programs can play out in reality.

The Kenya budget task force: focusing on process and decision-making

An earlier experience in Kenya also highlights how the Bank can respond with new approaches when faced by knotty problems. In Kenya, the agricultural project portfolio in the mid-1980s faced a host of frustrating problems, seemingly disconnected and resistant to efforts to resolve them. A common thread, it finally emerged, was a series of major flaws in how the government budget worked; funds did not reach the field on time. Multi-sectoral programs could not be well designed and managed, and forward budgeting worked only in theory. While the budget process was not the domain of agricultural project staff in the Bank or their Kenyan counterparts, explorations with a highly qualified consultant resoundingly confirmed the importance of these financial aspects of program management. A program was worked out involving a two-year task force exercise through a partnership between the Bank and different government departments, simultaneously recommending practical and immediate process improvements and working to identify long-term reforms. The results exceeded all expectations as the working group tackled and solved a succession of relatively small but significant obstacles that allowed several project plans to advance far better and more speedily.

The Kenya budget task force was a little noticed part of Kenya's structural adjustment program at the time, attracting limited attention because it seemed too focused on process, and not enough on outcomes. But the kind of work and partnership involved was a harbinger of an area that has taken on critical importance for the Bank: public expenditure management reviews. Following the money from policy to implementation, and dealing with the nuts and bolts of how processes facilitate or hinder development programs are both essential parts of governance and institutional and capacity reform.

Reputational risk, sins of "omission" and "commission": the East Asia operational risk review

Even as the East Asia crisis was receding, a major new challenge confronted the World Bank's East Asia leaders and the Bank overall. What began as an unexpected protest against what had appeared, from the Bank perspective, a fairly routine agricultural project in Western China erupted as a crisis that divided the Bank's board and management, created tensions in the Bank's important partnership with China, and forced a rethinking of how the Bank assessed risk and implemented an elaborate battery of safeguard policies. The Bank's Western China project was the subject of intense review by the Bank's Inspection Panel which responded to a complaint that came on the verge of formal board consideration of the program, raising serious questions about Bank performance but also highlighting how complex the underlying

issues were. After the Bank had invested huge financial and managerial resources in endeavoring to correct the shortfalls in performance
(above all in implementing environmental and social assessment and
safeguards), the Chinese government, fed up with the controversy and
high costs of remedial measures, withdrew its request for the Bank to
finance the project, and proceeded with its own resources.[5]

In the wake of this painful and demanding experience, Jean-Michel
Severino, then Bank vice president for East Asia, asked for a full
review of the risks entailed in the Bank's work across the East Asia
region: what other unseen issues might be lurking? He was motivated
by the fact that the World Bank had not predicted at all the critiques
of the China project, and by the heavy reputational, administrative,
and financial burdens that the experience had entailed. The concern
was not to avoid all risk—taking risks is an essential part of development work—but to learn from the experience about the Bank's propensity to blind spots. The result was a comprehensive review of all
World Bank countries and technical sectors (like transport, agriculture
and education), involving a team composed of Bank staff and outside
specialists, including human rights specialists (a rare feature in World
Bank operations).

The Special Operational Review, as it was termed, was demanding,
but it opened many new avenues of insight. It highlighted how patchy
and incomplete the World Bank's political analysis had been (a continuing conundrum for the Bank as it deliberately eschewed political
engagement yet was caught in the mangle when political problems
arose), and how often the Bank simply did not take into account
outside knowledge (in this case about how the former Tibetan regions
of China were seen) in any systematic fashion. The review highlighted
the need for more creative social and political assessments by country,
sector, and project, and the need for positive efforts to broaden partnerships with civil society organizations, including those most critical
of the Bank. It framed the issue of how the Bank saw its role, not only
in terms of what faults it might commit where it did not follow its
policies and risked causing active harm (sins of commission) but also
its failures to act on important matters where it might with effort have
found the opportunity (sins of omission). None of this was new, but
the reviews (conducted two years in succession) underscored the
importance of opening up the shaded portions of World Bank operations. Perhaps most significant, the situation posed the challenge of
how the Bank should consider its role in the far less technical, more
complex and political world of the contemporary era, and highlighting
the implications of not acting because its mandate and instruments

were not clear. As an illustration, many in the Bank were concerned about and discussed two major social challenges in East Asia: trafficking of girls and the difficult challenges faced by migrant laborers, but they rarely if ever acted on their concerns. The operational review suggested that the Bank should make more concerted efforts to look for paths to action.

Civil society approaches the Bank's doors: 10,000 unhappy birthday cards

In 2004 the World Bank quietly marked the sixtieth anniversary of its founding. Its critics also took note, and one of their efforts entailed collecting, worldwide, cards that wished the Bank an unhappy birthday. The organizers of the campaign discussed with their counterparts inside the civil society unit at the Bank how to deliver the cards, in a way that would respectfully underscore the message they carried.

Organizers handed over the 10,000 or so cards (in several large mailbags) to a Bank representative during a publicized event just outside the main entrance. Bank staff then sifted and read the cards (though many were printed forms), summarized their messages, and passed those on to managers. The cards themselves, however, languished in the corner of an office until the Bank's librarians agreed that they could be housed in the mine in Pennsylvania where World Bank archives are stored.

The birthday card campaign illustrated two aspects of World Bank operations today: first, the Bank's continuing and usually cordial interchange with civil society organizations, including fierce critics; and second, the ongoing "battle of communications" that the somewhat ungenerous birthday wishes reflected—as they reflected the negative images of the Bank held by very diverse people in different parts of the world. These images are a far cry from the positive, confident picture of the World Bank that its web site and public relations projects.

Directing funds to communities ravaged by HIV/AIDS

The HIV/AIDS pandemic was identified in 1981, and its deadly impact was obvious by the late 1980s. Nonetheless, responses commensurate with the needs were painfully slow in the making, both because of the insidious nature of the disease, which defied simple solutions and required changes in personal behavior—never a simple matter, and because denial of the AIDS threat was widespread despite compelling evidence of suffering and disastrous projections. Over 33 million people today live with HIV/AIDS.

Only in 1996 did the World Bank launch a major Africa-wide response, known as the Multicountry AIDS Program (MAP). MAP provided for a series of country-tailored and -led programs that both strengthened government health departments across the board and channeled funds to communities and NGOs. In parallel, two other major programs were also launched: the multi-stakeholder Global Fund to Fight AIDS, Tuberculosis and Malaria, and the US government's President's Emergency Program to fight AIDS (PEPFAR). The tables had turned: financing was no longer the binding constraint it had been. Nonetheless, a common complaint that persists to this day is that funding too often does not reach those who need it most: small entities working in communities with limited means and often weak institutional capacity.

The challenge is a monumental one, as it involves hundreds of thousands of communities and institutions, most not created specifically to work on HIV/AIDS. And the World Bank is a wholesale organization, supporting programs at the national level, and is not equipped to respond directly to communities in its bread and butter work. Yet the Bank's MAP projects and others along similar lines carried a promise to do what was required to respond to the crisis. This commitment led the Bank into numerous special efforts, including workshops on designing local programs to address HIV/AIDS, new instruments and procedures for combating the epidemic, successive evaluations of experience, and communications campaigns to alert people to the nature of the disease and preventive measures.

One such effort involved two workshops, in Addis Ababa and Accra in Ethiopia, for interfaith leader teams from 16 African countries, to help them navigate the procedures in place in each country for obtaining funding for community initiatives. These popular workshops targeted an essential group—faith communities, which are deeply engaged in addressing AIDS and its devastating social impacts—and met a real need. The difficulty in mobilizing funds for follow-on workshops in other countries, however, highlights limits on what the World Bank can do within its own administrative resources, particularly when several countries and civil society stakeholders are concerned.

Looking for better aid coordination in Mozambique

After an uneasy beginning (largely ideological in nature), the World Bank came to play a critical role in Mozambique as it emerged from civil wars in 1992 and faced an endless list of demands for development.

The Bank mobilized its full battery of potential support—analysis, lending, experience in various social sectors, debt advice, and capacity building and training. The Bank also organized a Consultative Group, as it became clear that mobilizing external support would present continuing challenges, and that coordination among the many agencies operating in Mozambique was an urgent need. The small World Bank office in Maputo was sorely stretched, and the country team was unable to respond to all of the numerous needs. However, overall the Bank's mobilization to support Mozambique in its transitional phase was dynamic, creative, and ambitious.

The aid coordination process proved to be particularly demanding—above all because the government was overwhelmed with the tasks it faced and had inherited weak capacity. Confronted with conflicting advice from different development partners, jealousies among them, and changing teams and roles, public officials often responded in exasperation. The formal Consultative Group meetings were held in Paris (as was the norm at the time), and served an important role in galvanizing economic analysis and financial support, but these annual gatherings were cumbersome and costly and clearly did not meet the need for dynamic daily interactions.

The history of aid coordination in Mozambique illustrates the evolution of thinking and action on that front at the time. That history entailed a rather messy progression toward local aid coordination groups involving interested donors, with leadership shifting toward the government in fits and starts; genuine efforts to coordinate the plethora of separate grant and lending operations and reviews of project portfolios; work to address obvious overlaps in areas such as procurement of goods and services and financial management, which placed burdens on the government; and an increasing openness in these processes to NGOs, which had acted quite independently but now sought admission to the aid coordination process. Operations in sectors came to replace investments in individual projects; leadership responsibilities among development partners became clearer in politicized areas like election monitoring and local government reform; and the World Bank became active in major arenas like health and education sector reforms and revamping of the banking system.

Dialogue across cultures: the Fès Forum

The World Bank provided support (tiny in scale for the Bank but large by other standards) from its budget and staff for five years to encourage the development of a highly unusual forum. President James Wolfensohn's deep interest in culture and music led to his personal (not financial) patronage of the Fès Festival of Global Sacred Music, an annual event held in Morocco designed to promote understanding and appreciation of cultural diversity. The parallel Fès Forum was launched in 2001 to bring together people from very different backgrounds and disciplines to discuss tensions and knotty problems around globalization. The forum had the unusual idea that even people with sharply conflicting views would communicate differently and more meaningfully against the inspiring backdrop of music that illustrated the real value of human diversity. The World Bank's engagement in the forum was also a product of a project to support the ancient city of Fès, designed to both fight the poverty there and preserve a cultural treasure.

The World Bank's presence in Fès raised eyebrows (not least within the World Bank itself) because it went so sharply against traditional images of a technocratic institution focused on economic issues alone. But the Bank's involvement flowed naturally from its relationship with Morocco, which was playing an important role in debates on globalization, by offering an unusual and creative setting for dialogue, and from the Bank's growing engagement with a wide range of disciplines and civil society actors. The Fès Forum represented a rich and demanding opportunity for the Bank to listen to very different voices, and to explore ideas on topics like identity, reconciliation, changes within Islam, and education.

Opening doors for women at the World Bank

It was by no means obvious in the early 1970s that calls from World Bank governors for a more diverse staff and leadership included recruiting more women, nor was it obvious what such change would entail. Because the Bank is an international organization, the legal paths followed in several countries, including the United States, to break ancient patterns of discrimination were not open. Change thus came slowly, amid a prevailing assumption that it would occur in its own good time as women earned their place through education and experience. The understanding that change could not come without models and leadership took time to percolate. Bank leaders and staff members increasingly appreciated that issues for women were important to development, but women at the Bank themselves were reluctant to confine their work to issues for women. The prospect was for more slow, deliberate change.

The pace of change quickened, however, because of concerted action by women working for the Bank. Nancy Barry led a survey that gave Bank managers something their culture and minds could not ignore: solid data. Women worked together to press the case for specific policy changes, and to provide models for what could be done in the face of assumptions (voiced quite openly) that women could not work in certain countries, or represent the World Bank at senior government levels. As women were appointed first as division chiefs, then to director positions, the group of leaders met regularly to support each other. Mentoring arrangements were active and creative. Change still came relatively slowly but it became inexorable, and affected more than the profile of the Bank. It contributed to overall shifts in managerial style, and also to deeply rooted attention to gender issues—not as an add-on, but as a central feature of Bank operations in many, though not all, cases.

This short, positive vignette makes the case that change from within is possible, and often necessary. It requires solid information, concerted effort, a strong human touch, and patience.

Introducing new approaches and partners: dialogue with faith organizations

An enduring criticism of the World Bank is that it takes on too much (some refer to it as a "mission creep"), and in response leaders within and outside the institution often pour cold water on new initiatives; one creative Bank leader once remarked that if he mentioned a new idea, the plants outside his office began to wither. The risk of dispersion of effort is real, and the Bank is not good at ending programs that are under way, or adapting them in fundamental ways as time goes on. Nonetheless, in a fast-changing world, a negative attitude toward new ideas is dangerous. The difficult path of a demanding but important initiative—to strengthen dialogue with faith institutions worldwide—is a case in point.

In 1998 James Wolfensohn launched a dialogue process together with George Carey, then Archbishop of Canterbury. Their early meetings with leaders of the world's major faith traditions demonstrated the depth of misunderstanding among all actors, but also strong common interests, and, still more, that all were directly engaged in fighting poverty and promoting social justice. The group agreed on a modest program of dialogue supported by a joint initiative, termed the World Faiths Development Dialogue (WFDD). The stiff opposition that this initiative encountered in 2000 at the Bank was a sobering reminder of the sensitivities in today's world on the specific subject of religion, and of the unease among many Bank executive directors about crossing lines they saw as separating economic and social policies from the realm of politics. The association of the effort with James Wolfensohn's personal leadership left the initiative open to neglect when Paul Wolfowitz took over as Bank president in 2005. However, Paul Wolfowitz, motivated by his political science background and appreciation of religion's strategic role in human security issues, made an affirmative decision to undertake a two-prong approach to the faith and development work, relying in the future more heavily on the outside WFDD, now based in Washington, DC and retained a small anchor unit within the World Bank. In the future, given the increasing interest in these issues, the team within the Bank will likely grow to accommodate increased need.

Dialogue between the World Bank and faith organizations could take many forms, and it needs to be deeply anchored in individual countries. However, given the global significance of religious forces in pivotal development arenas such as health, education, and social cohesion, ignoring religion should simply not be an option. The World Bank's difficult path in engaging in a thoughtful review of how this promising dialogue should proceed illustrates some of the perils confronting a large organization with an immensely complex governance structure, and multiple competing demands for attention and action.

Summary

The World Bank, as a global institution, working in widely different countries and regions, with a long time horizon, and with a mandate covering development, reconstruction, and social justice and equity, is involved in an extraordinary range of issues, situations, and partnerships. The 16 cases in this chapter illustrate the complex technical, political, social and ethical issues that confront the Bank. They also illustrate its multi-sectoral challenge—of trying to forge sensitive and effective links among very different issues, disciplines and institutions in situations that span highly technical issues (cattle ranching, managing community development, handling the aftermath of devaluation), and the broad socio-political issues involved in designing policies and programs to fight poverty. The Bank works through a wide variety of instruments, some of them formal (loans, reports, conferences), some far less so. It addresses specific macroeconomic and sectoral challenges like banking reform but it also needs to take into account issues like governance, corruption, the role of the underground economy, and how it communicates its views and works with others whose perspectives may be quite different. The Bank works best when it is able to bring together the different elements into an integrated program and when it can set its actions both in a technical and in a pragmatic perspective informed by ethical considerations and thoughtful political analysis.

6 The World Bank and its critics

The World Bank is known in many circles primarily through the reflected image projected by its critics. The Bank is no stranger to controversy; its large size, the weight of its influence in many situations, and the controversial power structure that rules it (above all the dominant voice of richer countries), in particular, give rise to a quite extraordinary range of questions about its governance (including its very legitimacy), its policies, its operations, its management, and its culture. While voices and protest were raised from an early date, questioning the mandate and philosophy of the new institution as well as its practical actions and approach, these were generally fairly polite, and the Bank lived through a long period when it was fairly insulated from critical voices; a pattern of complacency set in, extending to the early 1990s. The civil society revolution globally, and its engagement with the World Bank, first through environmental issues (in the 1980s) but with an ever-widening agenda, changed this complacency forever.

The peak period of controversy came around the time of the Bank's fiftieth anniversary, in 1994, and in ensuing years an almost siege mentality gripped the institution and its critics, symbolized in the high chain-link fences that surrounded Bank buildings, especially during important meetings. The era of protests and intense criticism has given way to a more complex pattern, more decentralized and working through many channels including media and the internet. The Bank has become far more open to and engaged with a wide range of outside critics (as well as allies) while the coalesced protest movement of the peak protest years has reshaped in more complex forms, often more focused on specific issues. The small groups of protesters of the 1990s who looked to violent means and spurred the Bank to close its doors and surround itself with fences have been eclipsed by actual and feared threats from terrorist groups, so the physical security barriers for the Bank (like many other public institutions) have different motivations than when they were first introduced. Nonetheless, despite the changing and multiple forms of protest and criticism, overall the World Bank operates now in a far less secure, far less confident, and far more complex external environment than the simpler institution of the past.

The central questions at issue turn around accountability: who is accountable to whom, for what, with what authority, and by what measures? This in turn raises the issue not only of how the World Bank relates to its member countries and the different parts of their governments but also to the array of civil society institutions that seek to hold it to account, to other global institutions with different mandates and governance (including articulate critics of the Bank within the UN system), and, in the final analysis, to the poor communities who are its professed focus and *raison d'être*. This highly complex and interrelated set of concerns have been addressed by thoughtful observers, prominent among them Jonathan Fox and David Brown, and John Clark (who himself played a central role in shaping the Bank's early policies on civil society).[1] They provide a nuanced account, exploring the origins of transnational civil society organizations, their links to the grassroots movements that represent the people directly concerned, and the complex patterns of World Bank response, which they see as made up both of fundamental shifts in policy and skillful coping and cosmetic adjustments. Both point to a long agenda of topics for further research, dialogue, and action.

This chapter explores the range of critics and criticisms of the Bank, first through the lens held up by the civil society institutions which have brought such fundamental changes in the operating environment, and second, through five different groups of critiques: (a) that the Bank represents empire, or the "project" of extending the influence of the rich and powerful across the world; (b) that the Bank follows an economic theology that is narrow and attuned to the world's rich, not the poor communities it is supposed to serve; (c) that the effects of Bank policies and operations (especially infrastructure construction and macroeconomic reforms) hurt poor communities, (d) that the Bank fails to take ethical considerations sufficiently into account, in pursuing the goal of equity and global justice, in fighting against corrupt and undemocratic regimes, and in working for basic human rights, and, (e) that the Bank is still, despite its efforts to open up, too closed, hard to understand, and, overall, an enigma. The final section reflects on how the Bank responds to these critiques, in constructive and unconstructive ways, and how the critiques have changed and are changing the Bank.

Framing critiques and issues

Criticisms of the Bank take a wide variety of forms, and the topics of protest and response cannot be understood without seeking some logical ordering among them. Some critiques involve fundamental questioning of the very existence and motives of the institution: the names of two protest groups, *50 Years Is Enough*, and *Abolish the Bank* gives a pretty clear message about their stance (they were established in advance of the World Bank's fiftieth anniversary in 1994).[2] Other critics advocate and pressure for deep reforms of the international financial architecture seen as represented or promoted by the Bank, and of the overall development process. Most critiques, however, address specific issues and actions (such as policies on debt, approach to indigenous peoples, gender policies, policies on banking, resettlement policies) in a spirit of reform.

The most visible criticisms have been the mass mobilizations that were so dramatic in the late 1990s and early years of the new century. These took many forms, but included many large demonstrations that were usually but not always peaceful; some were angry in tone, while others took on almost a street theater quality, with dragons and puppets used to dramatize the message and capture media imagination. These protests reached a crescendo after intensive clashes during a succession of international meetings, including the annual meetings of the World Bank and the International Monetary Fund (IMF). The resulting siege environment prompted people involved with various meetings to sleep at their World Bank offices; meeting sites including the World Bank headquarters were surrounded by nine-foot-high chain-link fences for several city blocks, and sleepy delegates were asked to arrive before dawn so that police convoys could usher them into the fortress complex.

Alongside the demonstrations and protests, and arguably much more significant, is the elaborate engagement between the World Bank and myriad critics through its complex governance processes—whether the governors representing all Bank member countries, the smaller Board of Directors, or, increasingly, the parliamentary bodies in the home country of each Bank governor. The Bank's policies are constantly under scrutiny, increasingly through a formal phase of consultations on programs and projects that often results in significant changes in design and timing. Recent consultations (2006–7) on the World Bank's governance strategy are a case in point.

And last but not least is the constant battle and engagement of ideas. One continuous flow of activity focuses on policy reviews and task forces, some commissioned by the Bank itself and others generated by outside groups (recent examples are the World Commission on Dams, debates about resettlement, to extractive industries and institutional integrity). Innumerable intellectual commentaries also appear in books, articles, web sites, and tracts; and media coverage of these critiques and the policies and actions of the World Bank is often lively and extensive. Some of the Bank's most effective and often scathing critics are former officers and staff members, who know well the "skeletons in the closet" and can navigate the lexicon of the institution.[3]

The leading critiques can be organized into five major concerns:[4]

- Doubts surrounding the Bank's overall role and structure, meaning US dominance reflecting global imbalances of economic power, the Bank's undemocratic governance set-up, and the institution's size, breadth of activity, and reach.
- The Bank's economic ideology or theology, meaning that it adheres to narrow economic models in its work.
- The impact of Bank policies and operations, including displacement of populations and environmental damage resulting from individual projects; the effects of policies such as recovery of investment costs for services like health, water and energy, and direct results of macroeconomic policy implementation, such as debt burdens and misdirected economic reform.
- Concerns about the Bank's ethics, including the integrity of its staff, the effectiveness of its action against corruption, and its relationships with governments that arguably do not represent their people or support basic human rights.
- The enigma of the World Bank itself, which is hard to understand and thus often poorly understood.

The full barrage of critiques and counter-critiques are the subject of numerous thoughtful works. One continuing source of commentary is the Bretton Woods Project, whose bimonthly updates are always thoughtful and often insightful (if almost universally negative and sometimes somewhat jaundiced in tone).[5]

Three illustrative books provide some insight into the nature and direction of criticism. William Easterly's *The Elusive Quest for Growth* is the product of a disillusioned World Bank economist who understands well many pitfalls of the overall development business, though he offers few solutions. Susan George and Fabrizio Sabelli's critique of the World Bank goes for the jugular in its portrayal of misguided policies in a global setting, as does Catherine Caulfield's work.[6]

Among critical documents repeatedly cited is the 2000 report of the International Financial Institutions Advisory Commission (also known as the Meltzer commission), created by the US Congress. The commission urged changes in the direction of the World Bank (as well as the IMF), including a cutback in activities in middle-income countries and a shift from loan to grant terms.[7] The long-time and respected director general of the Bank's Operations Evaluation Department, Robert Picciotto (now retired), can always be counted on for pithy and provocative commentary (see, for example, his recent report tying human security to development).[8]

This chapter does not purport to summarize or assess the full gamut of critiques. Rather, it explores the five core areas of criticism noted above, to illustrate the arguments of those who seek to change the Bank or hold up its work to scrutiny.

The imperial Bank

Perhaps the angriest and most fundamental criticisms of the World Bank are those that regard the international financial institutions (IFIs) (particularly the IMF and World Bank) through the lens of geopolitics, and thus as a blunt instrument of US hegemony and power. This vision often encompasses other rich countries, and thus sees the IFIs as an extension of the colonial power of the past century. The World Bank is portrayed as serving the political and economic interests of the wealthy and powerful, seeking to increase their wealth at the expense of poor countries and poor people. It is described as putty in the hands of multinational companies, serving their interests by paving the way for private investment.

The perception is sobering because it is vehemently held in fairly broad circles, and because—as with virtually all perceptions—it contains strands of truth. It is discouraging because the international institutions were established precisely to avoid the pitfalls of narrow national policies. National interests, including economic and security motivations, do creep (and sometimes plunge) into decision-making in the IFIs, but they are usually tempered by a cooperative spirit, and a genuine if perhaps insufficient concern with poverty and social justice that pervade the institutions. The pragmatic idealism that dominates the culture of the IFIs accepts an element of national jockeying and interest, but tries to keep the poverty and development focus at the fore.

More difficult to address is what some call the "democracy deficit" of the World Bank, by which is meant its voting system, which gives more weight to countries that contribute greater shares of the funding.

Figure 6.1 Illustrating governance debates and weighted voting.

Without question this system gives wealthier countries far more power than the poor countries the World Bank aims to serve (Table 3.2, p. 78).

This governance system is deeply embedded, and while some adjustments in nations' voting power have been made over time, these changes are largely at the margin. Discussions of further changes, such as those at the annual meetings of the IFIs in Singapore in September 2006, focus on shifts in economic strength that justify changing share allocations in favor of middle-income countries.

Efforts to strengthen the influence of poorer countries (especially those in Africa) tend to take a path of advocating greater "voice," by which is meant procedural and attitude changes that privilege the views of those who are directly affected by policies, even if they have fewer votes. Such efforts rarely impress critics of the governance structure, who see them as insufficient and entirely within a flawed system. The tradition of consensus decision-making on the Bank's Board of Directors—which includes representatives from smaller and poor nations—partly reflects such long-standing concerns, and a genuinely cooperative response to the imbalance of power. Rarely spoken but fundamental to the debate is concern that IDA's ability to raise funds stems in significant part from a voting system that ensures that the interests of the financiers are decisive in cases of controversy. The governance debate is likely to continue for the foreseeable future, but at this stage no concrete proposals for major overhaul are even on the table.

A final element behind the "imperial critique" is the sheer size and reach of the World Bank, which for some means that the institution holds excessive and unhealthy power over the fate of poor countries, particularly those that have no choice but to engage with the Bank if they wish to survive crisis and secure financing to support their development. The characterization by Denis Goulet, a pioneer in development ethics, of development experts as "one-eyed giants" reflects this critique of an institution too large, protected, and insulated to appreciate the realities of poverty and inequity, and thus help overcome them. Proposals to end the practice of making funding conditional on macroeconomic reforms address this issue, though it is hard to imagine a financial institution making loans or grants without clear agreement on how they will be used. Other proposed remedies include relying more heavily on regional banks to finance development, creating new institutions like the Bank of the South suggested by Hugo Chávez, president of Venezuela, or breaking the World Bank up into smaller and thus hopefully more nimble and responsive entities.

Another important strand of criticism decries "mission creep," seeing a World Bank that cannot say no and thus steadily expands its purview. This critique sees the Bank stretched to a point of ineffectiveness, that also undermines the capacity of other institutions that were designed to act in the fields the World Bank invades. Jessica Einhorn, former managing director of the World Bank, set out such arguments thoughtfully in an article entitled "The World Bank's Mission Creep" in *Foreign Affairs* in 2001.[9] The problem is real; witness the Bank's extraordinarily wide range of activities today and well-known difficulty in cutting back on any activity on which it has embarked. Also real, however, are urgent calls from shareholders for the Bank to take on new roles, some quite far afield from its formal mandate, such as administering funds on behalf of the Global Fund for AIDS, Tuberculosis and Malaria, leading efforts to plan for an avian flu epidemic, and coordinating programs in post-armed conflict situations. The need for a comprehensive approach linking all strands of the development process is also compelling. The days when it was plausible to argue that the World Bank should stick to infrastructure are long gone.

Economic theology

Two very different views of the World Bank's approaches to economic work are common. One sees a highly skilled, disciplined, altruistic institution that looks with objectivity and fresh eyes at each country's situation, bringing to bear the best global knowledge (this view is notably centered among Bank staff and its governors). The other perceives an institution that has a clear economic ideology that some term neoliberal, and which applies that ideological vision across the board, with little adaptation and little real room for discussion with those affected (this is the view of a significant group of critics). "Washington Consensus" is a term applied to a set of specific economic reforms seen as a mandatory recipe whose merits are widely debated, even as the economist who coined the term (John Williamson) protests that there was never such a consensus, and that the "recipe" image is a distorted one. The ideological vision of the World Bank is troubling, as it is difficult to debate, and different parties tend to be set in their own perspectives. The two narratives—much as they are presented here as a caricature—reflect considerable reality, and schools of thought that remain far apart.

Positions between these two clearly exist, and active debate among economists on this range of views is a fundamental aspect of the World Bank's daily life. Indeed, the field of economics has numerous schools, and many are represented within the World Bank, which aspires to remain at the cutting edge. Countless Bank publications and conferences present widely different viewpoints, and debate can be heated and open. To take just one example, Robert Wade (London School of Economics) argues in many Bank-hosted settings that the World Bank's economic work fails to take fully into account the complex realities of income distribution in its oversimplified vision of poverty matters, and the record of the most successful East Asian tiger countries in protecting their industry from foreign competition. Such topics are under continuous discussion within the Bank, and are a healthy sign of intellectual rigor and curiosity. A 2006 evaluation of the World Bank's research work from 1998 to 2005, commissioned by the Bank and led by Angus Deaton (Princeton University), affirmed the breadth and general high quality of the Bank's economic work. Still, it raised rather troubling questions about how far its research and findings are skewed toward positions the Bank has already adopted or wishes to advocate.[10]

The effects of policies and projects

Many criticisms of the World Bank address the direct, on the ground consequences of its investments in individual projects, and its advice on economic policy, particularly when it makes assistance conditional on specific economic reforms. The most organized and intensive project critiques have focused on environmental damage, and several specific cases have plainly changed Bank policies and approaches in fundamental ways. These include prominently development schemes in the Brazilian Amazon region, and the large Narmada Dam project in India.

The criticisms have centered on the perceived failure of the World Bank to take into account environmental damage from forest cutting (in Amazonia) and displacement of many thousands of people (Narmada), though critics have also leveled a host of other criticisms of project selection, design, and process. Virtually all dam construction projects are now subject to extraordinarily intense scrutiny, to a point where governments with options for securing financing elsewhere are likely to eschew World Bank involvement, seen as more trouble than it is worth.

Also subject to careful review as a result of external pressures are projects that involve indigenous peoples, as the effects of insensitive design were seen as highly damaging. From a string of project failures and consequent criticism—both internal and external—the World Bank has changed its approach to involve local people in planning projects, and has introduced far more rigorous and extensive social analysis. These few illustrations are the tip of a large iceberg of debate about the several thousand projects the World Bank finances. One result of the process of opening the Bank to scrutiny is that documents on projects are publicly available fairly early in the preparation process, as a way to encourage debate and hopefully improve design.

How the Bank advises governments, and the effects of this advice, is the subject of active internal and external discussion. Such debate concerns broad macroeconomic advice and above all how policy reform is implemented, but the Bank also is involved on a daily basis with specific recommendations across many sectors of activities. Most are linked to the financial facts of life for institutions and programs and thus touch on subsidies for water and electricity use, irrigation charges, and health, education, and water supply fees. There are two main strands of criticism: first, that the Bank's advice is dogmatic and insensitive and thus inappropriate to individual circumstances; and second, that it too often imposes these conditions without consulting sufficiently with those involved. Many Bank staff see both arguments as having merit, but also contend that the institution significantly reformed its approaches some years back.

Particularly intensive and frustrating (for all concerned) discussions have focused on Bank-supported structural adjustment programs (described in Chapter 2), which aimed to support far-ranging economic reforms. Critics often describe these programs in unambiguous terms as harming poor communities and people by cutting jobs, raising prices, and increasing fees for services, including education, health, and water. Many studies and reviews by both the Bank and its critics provide very different narratives of what the Bank tried to do, what actually happened, why countries have often failed to follow the intended path, and where recommended economic reforms have succeeded in transforming a country's prospects. What is clear is that the dialogue about many such experiences is patently insufficient, and that cases vary so widely that simplistic images produce more noise than light.

Spotlight on ethics

Critics of the World Bank often present their views in moral and ethical terms—with inferences about the intentions of those involved, and the relative moral weight of differing positions. The World Bank, in contrast, is characterized by a highly technical ethos, and above all the technical language it uses to present issues. The word ethics, until recently, barely figured in its vocabulary. The World Bank has always viewed itself as highly virtuous, setting the highest ethical standards for both individual and institutional comportments. However, this ethical sense was rarely articulated, and the Bank's virtue and staff honesty were often essentially taken for granted, with fairly limited oversight. The apparatus of procedures for financial management and procurement of goods and services, and, more recently, a battery of "safeguard policies" to ensure that lending adheres to strict policies, were seen as guaranteeing honesty and underpinning integrity. The Bank's unease in discussing corruption over many years (hence its nickname, the "c" word) resulted from both pressures to avoid political engagement and an assumption that the problem could be dealt with by technical means, which were not served by open discussion.

Lack of explicit recognition within the World Bank's organizational culture of the many ethical dimensions of its work, coupled with inevitably uneven application of rules, opened the door to criticism. The Bank seemed tone deaf to many ethical arguments, leading, for example, to particular tensions with faith communities, for whom ethics is an essential part of their approach and language. Likewise, human rights activists have been and remain frustrated in their dealings with the World Bank, because it has hesitated even to state publicly that it supports human rights. The Bank argues that it advances human rights through its policies and actions, but cannot engage in what it sees as the political aspects of many facets of human rights.

Figure 6.2 Illustrating the aftermath of debates about governance under Wolfowitz.

Policies in all these arenas are undergoing important changes. The World Bank prides itself on being a world leader in openly and actively fighting corruption (as it has done for more than a decade), for example, and more recently its leaders have been more forthright in advocating and acting for human rights. However, the Bank continues to operate within the confines of its Articles of Agreement, which make the "p" word—politics—a constant source of sensitivity. The circumstances around Paul Wolfowitz' departure in June 2007 put the full range of ethical challenges under a powerful microscope (Figure 6.2). Debates are likely to continue.

The enigma

A final set of critiques reflects the fact that the World Bank is too often rather enigmatic and very hard to penetrate and understand.

The Bank is immensely complex, composed of numerous parts and assuming different shapes and forms in different situations. The Bank's organizational structure and practices exacerbate this complexity, particularly the matrix structure, which aims to ensure that teams form and reform as needs dictate, and the hierarchy (designed to be "flat" and not hierarchical), which distinguishes between leaders of countries and sectors, and defines sectors in a peculiarly Bank fashion. The detailed organization chart is impenetrable for most people, as it includes leaders, managers, and directors, for example. The Bank has, in addition, an extraordinary propensity for jargon and acronyms, which exacerbates the real and underlying complexity of both the issues at stake and its work. Finally, portals into the Bank to help outsiders find their way to the people and information they need are not well developed, poorly integrated, and hard to search.

These intrinsic complexities were compounded in the past by policies and practices of secrecy that shrouded most Bank work. The progression of documents through different stages of internal approval, from dirty white (unfinished) to white (mission draft), yellow (manager-approved), green (for discussion with a government), and grey or buff (official but not public) contributed to the mystery. Employees were supposed to release little information, even to government officials, leading, not unnaturally, to the common practice of managed leaks. As noted, the information policies of today are vastly different, and much Bank work is now in the public domain, accessible through public information centers and the Bank's extensive web site. Even so, many of the World Bank's procedures remain rather enigmatic and opaque to most observers.

The recent healthy changes in practices and information disclosure policies should make the World Bank somewhat less of an enigma. However, a long path lies ahead before the institution fulfills its stated desire for transparency and clarity.

The Bank's handling of and response to its critics

The World Bank often conveys the image that it is rather complacent, solidly established, and overconfident in its roles and work, but the present reality—that the institution is subject to an extraordinarily wide array of criticism—is never far from view.

The World Bank encounters its critics in many forums. It is in constant contact with a wide gamut of people and institutions in countries where it works, and the whys and hows behind specific World Bank actions and stands are always part of the dialogue. The Bank also forays increasingly into institutional and person-to-person contact with critics of many stripes, whether by issuing materials designed to allay what it sees as misunderstandings or engaging in debate and dialogue.

The World Bank also relies increasingly on survey instruments and systematic reviews of media coverage. Formal reviews of the World Bank by its members take many forms, including for example the 1990 US-sponsored Meltzer Commission, and continuing policy reviews by the Development Committee, an advisory group to the board of governors.[11]

The Bank makes growing use of advisory groups, some of which bring in well-known critics, to give one-time or continuing commentary. Examples include the Council of African Advisors, which met regularly with leaders of the Bank's Africa team for many years (similar councils advise Bank staff in other regions); the Anti Corruption Advisory Group for the East Asia Region; advisory groups on gender; and a council supporting the World Bank Institute (this is a small sample; there are many more). The Bank has its own formalized internal critics, notably the Independent Evaluation Group (IEG), which examines individual projects as well as the Bank's overall effectiveness; and the Quality Assurance Group (QAG), whose functions include a hard look at projects at the point of formal approval (see Chapter 3). In some respects the Bank is its own harshest critic, and few proposals go unscathed by what is commonly sharp questioning at all levels, though of course it depends on context to what extent the layers of critique are well integrated into the given proposal.

The manner of the Bank's response has changed markedly over time. For several decades, the Bank was subject to fairly sedate criticism, and its policy was essentially not to respond. This stance was somewhat imperious and disdainful of critics, and reflected the Bank's confidence that the storms would subside. Most documents were tightly held secrets, and Bank staff members were enjoined not to talk to media. (The Bank's position was that governments were responsible for representing their work with the Bank, and should thus handle media contacts themselves, with the Bank in a shadowy background.) The combination of protests directed at exposing information collected by the World Bank and its own analysis to public scrutiny, a general trend toward more open governance, and technological changes that have made dissemination far easier and secrets much harder to hold have revolutionized the situation.

The World Bank today is acutely conscious of the critiques and its public image. It can evince an aura of wounded dignity at times, in part the result of genuine bemusement at the anger of critics. The Bank is still better at explaining than at listening. Further, a widespread if somewhat risky response by staff to much external questioning of the World Bank is that the institution is simply misunderstood. But it is a rare Bank officer or employee who does not follow outside debates about the Bank with care, many engage directly in dialogue, and many do not hesitate to say that they often agree with the critics. The spectacle of the Bank's response to the leadership crisis in April–May 2007, when the performance and tenure of Paul Wolfowitz, the Bank's then president were in question, is revealing of an institution that, willingly or unwillingly, is almost entirely open to public scrutiny with its staff prepared to engage.

The response to public criticism takes many forms. It includes a fairly classic monitoring and messaged response from a media team with a strong public relations bent. (This function was professionalized particularly starting with the tenure of Mark Malloch Brown, later administrator of the United Nations Development Programme (UNDP) and deputy secretary general of the United Nations (UN).) In parallel, a large group of staff explicitly focus on civil society, with a small team working globally, and with staff members in most countries having explicit responsibilities for engaging with civil society organizations. In times of particular crisis (the African debt crisis in the 1980s and the East Asia financial crisis in 1998 would count among such instances), the Bank mobilizes special media teams.

The more important question is how external critiques change policy and practice. The answer falls under the frustrating heading of "it depends ... " There is no question that political attacks on the World Bank have important repercussions, some bringing positive change, others engendering resistance. The most significant example of both intellectual critique and moral mobilization leading to fundamental change is the civil society mobilization around debt, which reoriented dialogue about poor country debt and provided impetus and language for major changes in policy, approach, and financing for development.[12] Day-to-day interchange on issues and insights with outside observers are an essential part of the learning and adaptation that should be the norm for all institutions, especially the Bank, which carries momentous responsibilities for human welfare and security. What is more difficult to judge is whether the pace of change is sufficient, with the answers likely to vary widely among different observers.

What this complex pattern of debate, engagement, and dynamic change over the past two decades illustrates is the ferociously complex structure of accountability that is a central World Bank feature. The formal governance structure is already complex, involving governors representing 185 governments and the full accountability structure behind them. Supporting the US executive director, who represents the United States on the World Bank Executive Board and manages the Bank's relations with the US Congress, is a large job in itself, but it is mirrored in many other countries. Add to that the Bank's fundamental responsibility to its client governments, and, in those countries, to a wide variety of institutions, public and private, that have a direct interest in the Bank's work.

In addition, especially in recent years, the Bank's fundamental understanding is that it has a responsibility to speak and act for the poorest segments of the population. While this is often part of a coherent strategy agreed upon by a government and the Bank, on many occasions the Bank believes that its concern for poor citizens is stronger and more forthright than that of their own government, and sees its responsibility as taking up their cause. And on top of these actors comes the active engagement of many civil society groups, global and national, large and widely representative, and very special-purpose.

At times, to Bank staff members, it appears that—rather than the lack of accountability that some critics pose as the fundamental problem—they are accountable to everyone everywhere all the time. One colleague suggested that, given the maze of conflicting accountability requirements, he focuses on the impact of his actions on unborn generations as the central test. This is all well and good, but future generations will not judge results for a long time, and in the here and now plenty of voices will be raised in protest. A recent cartoon also reflects a concerned view of Bank staff and allies—that the controversies threaten to detract from the institution's capacity to respond to poor communities in the most effective manner (see Figure 6.3).

Summary

Many see the Bank as controversial and flawed, some speaking from direct experience and research, many more from complex yet partial reflected images of what the Bank does. The criticisms of the Bank vary widely, some fundamental and calling into questions its mandate and basic policies; more focusing on specific aspects of its policies like environmental protection, handling of indebtedness, governance, cost recovery, and approaches to indigenous peoples. Accountability—to whom, for what, and by what measures, lie at the heart of the debates and the response.

Concerns about the Bank can be categorized under five headings. First is a fear that the power of the wealthy countries means that the Bank's work furthers their interests and power and extends the notion of "empire" in a modern guise. The Bank's dominance by economists

Figure 6.3 Poverty and controversies illustrated.

and its seeming adherence to specific economic approaches and doctrines convey a sense that a unified theology (termed neoliberalism, or the Washington consensus) is at work. The effects of Bank policies and operations, especially through the social impact of infrastructure projects but also privatization and other reform measures are seen as detrimental. Finally, many find the Bank difficult to understand and to penetrate, and see it as enigmatic and aloof.

The Bank's response to the important critical voices came rather late, slowly, and often reluctantly, but in many respects the environment of protest and criticism has transformed the institution, opening it up to dialogue, prying open its secret documents, and forcing new communications and listening approaches. Nonetheless, the Bank still has far to go to engage its critics effectively and to respond to their many legitimate concerns.

7 Looking ahead
Challenges facing the World Bank

The World Bank's complex mandate and global reach do not lend themselves to simple approaches (however tempting it is to look to three point solutions). While the Bank's poverty mandate remains salient and forward-looking, the institution faces the prominent challenges of contributing to global development agendas while remaining relevant to client governments in a context where they have significantly more choices in seeking support, whether from bilateral donors or private enterprise. There are significant tensions among different paths, and thus strategic choices are a continuing preoccupation of leaders and observers alike.

At the most fundamental level, will and should the institution grow in size and power, or should it shrink? Should its mandate continue to expand as new global challenges emerge, or should the Bank be far more selective in what it takes on, and even withdraw from significant areas where it is now engaged? How central a player will the World Bank be in the architecture of global institutions dedicated to promoting development? How much finance will it be able to mobilize, and on what terms? How will it use those funds, and how will it ensure, in turn, that recipients use them well? What about the World Bank's advisory and advocacy roles—how large should they be, and how should they be organized?

How central a priority will fighting poverty be in the future for client and donor countries alike, and what will that mean in practice for the Bank's operations? How will the World Bank address the challenges of equity among and within nations, an issue with wide repercussions across the global landscape, including in the global giants of Brazil, South Africa, India, Russia, Indonesia, and China? Which regions should have priority in the use of funds? How should the institution—as part of the broader international community—deal with the intrinsic difficulties of working successfully in weak and failing states? How should the institution deal with flagging interest among middle-income countries in borrowing from the Bank?

These and other questions come up again and again in discussions about the World Bank's future—both inside and outside the institution. This chapter sketches out these leading issues, some of which are hardy perennials that always appear on the agenda, while others are fresh or transformed questions that present new challenges.

Comprehensive or selective?

Discussions about the future of the World Bank inevitably begin and end with questions about its size and scope. The institution's scale of operations obviously reflects its mandate: the work it is expected to do, its role *vis-à-vis* other actors, and the resources it is able to mobilize.

The debate runs along familiar lines. The ambition of some is for an expanded leadership and coordination role for the World Bank, reflecting the comprehensive understanding of development challenges that has coalesced in recent years. Those adhering to this school see the Bank as well endowed by experience, resources, and potential fairness and objectivity to play such a leadership role on a wide range of issues. This camp would place the Bank near the center of the development solar system. It holds that the World Bank is vitally needed as a leader and intellectual clearinghouse within an essential multilateral system—the only institution that can bring more order and direction into the rather unruly and multifaceted international development community.

Others take a much dimmer view of the Bank's potential for global coordination and leadership, and would work for a far more defined and selective vision—up to and including abolishing the institution altogether. This camp sees the World Bank variously as too powerful, too large, too cumbersome, fatally biased in its approach, and stifling the initiative of individual countries, the private sector, and other multilateral institutions. Some see the World Bank's proliferation of activities in widely different arenas (including reforming countries' legal systems, supporting polio vaccination, engaging in interfaith dialogue, and promoting cultural development) as undermining its core competencies and genuine excellence in economics and finance.

This debate obviously reflects contrasting views of global issues and institutions, as well as of the World Bank and its performance per se. The debate rests on different perceptions of private-sector versus public-sector roles in economies and societies, the place that civil society will and should occupy, whether international institutions should trump national governments in the world order, and how relations among nations—especially given today's unbalanced world—will and should evolve. What is a just order? And what will work? Prophetic visionaries take ideal global relations as a starting point, and would revamp global institutions to achieve that vision. Pragmatic idealists tend to start with what exists, absorb lessons from experience, and define specific objectives as a foundation for moving forward.

This somewhat abstract commentary leads quickly to practical questions and strategic choices for the World Bank. For example, should the World Bank and the IMF merge into a single institution with a clearly defined financial and economic mandate? Should the UN system—as a more democratic body overall—take on many responsibilities now handled by the World Bank? Or should the UN system, including the World Bank, be curtailed in size and mandate, leaving more scope for the private sector and national authorities? Is the system so broken that full-blown change is essential? Or is it actually working fairly well, requiring change only at the margins?

Many of these debates have a chicken-and-egg quality: if the Bank has the needed capacity and resources, it is likely to be invited to take on new tasks (as it did after the East Asian financial crisis of 1997–8 and the Asian tsunami of 2004). Recent experience has shown that, for better or worse, the World Bank is often the institution best equipped to respond to new challenges, so willy-nilly it embraces fresh functions. If, however, its resources and thus capacity are curtailed, the Bank will likely move more to the margins and into more limited and specialized roles.

The World Bank's future mandate and scope of activities are not entirely or even largely in its hands. They depend on how the global institutional architecture changes, and how other institutions, including the United Nations Development Programme (UNDP), nongovernmental organizations, and private companies, evolve. Knowledgeable observers of the World Bank usually view the competition that often develops among these actors as healthy—if with some trepidation—as it encourages both efficiency and excellence. However, competition can also dampen efforts by the Bank and others to harmonize and coordinate development efforts.

Money issues

The $100 billion question is what resources the world will need to end poverty, and, more specifically, to achieve the Millennium Development Goals (MDGs). By some reckonings (for example, the passionate advocacy of economist Jeffrey Sachs), nothing is more important than mobilizing large and regular flows of financing from rich to poorer nations to support development programs and rebalance the world.[1] Negotiations around replenishing funding for the International Development Association (IDA) are already grounded in the arithmetic of the needs of poor countries, as are discussions of world poverty in forums such as the G-8 meetings of leaders from industrial countries.

Greater financing to meet these needs would come in three essential forms: more public-sector support for direct development assistance, stepped-up private-sector investments and flows, and catalytic engagement by foundations and civil society. However, this approach raises four central concerns: how much money is needed, whether and to what extent funding is really the issue, what kinds of finance are required, and what terms for awarding it would be both workable and just.

The MDGs turned an old equation on its head. Instead of asking what rich and poor countries can afford or are willing to spend on economic and social development, the MDGs queried instead what it would cost to achieve core development objectives. Commitments emanating from the 2002 Monterrey summit on Financing for Development, and many rhetorical promises since then, have asserted that richer countries will indeed provide the needed funding, if poorer countries fulfill their part of the bargain with sound economic and social policies and good governance.

Several computations have been crystal clear that the needed funding would far exceed current aid flows, and even current commitments (though the details are open to question). Overseas development assistance totaled some $70 billion in 2006, while the need is for about twice that level.[2] Discussions during the first major review of progress on the MDGs, in 2005—and during the G-8 summit in Gleneagles, Scotland, and a UN summit later that year—reaffirmed the commitments of rich nations to increasing aid levels to the long-standing target of 0.7 percent of GDP.

Of course, these nations have not linked these promised aid flows specifically to the World Bank. However, resources at those levels would almost certainly mean significant involvement of the Bank. As the premier global financial institution, the Bank can inspire the confidence essential to raising the needed public and private funds and using them effectively. The World Bank already plays a central role in ensuring that wealthier nations continue to review their aid flows, and in advocating for more financial support for fighting poverty. The World Bank is therefore a key player in arguing for more financing for development.

However, nagging critiques cut to the quick of the entire argument for major increases in resource flows to poor nations. Exemplified today by former World Bank economist William Easterly, critics argue that existing aid and development models are so flawed that financing is usually misdirected, and that few if any magic solutions would allow rapid increases in spending to translate into results. Variations on this theme suggest that any funding involving public institutions is unlikely to be well directed and managed owing to corruption, above all, and that financing flowing from richer to poorer countries perpetuates exploitative patterns, especially if it comes with strings attached. Proponents of these arguments would call for curbing the World Bank's role within a shrunken global apparatus for development assistance.

The outrage of global poverty and widespread evidence that development programs can and often do succeed counter these pessimistic views. Still, the doubters and naysayers color the debates and heighten long-standing concerns that regular and generous aid flows have proved fickle, however compelling the arguments for development assistance. The unpredictability of funding has spurred some to respond by advancing a compelling and continued case for development aid. Witness, for example, Bono's remarkable leadership in arguing passionately for greater aid, and the One campaign, which aims to mobilize wide public support for scaling up development assistance to meet the needs.[3]

Development institutions, including the World Bank, are also responding to the challenges about aid effectiveness and needs with a highly disciplined focus on linking development financing to results, and a battery of new ways to ensure that funds are used honestly, with stout and effective measures to cut corruption. Such a dual strategy is essential, entailing energetic work to keep the case for increasing aid high on policy agendas (notably at G-8 meetings and UN summits, but also on domestic political agendas), and recognition that funding is only part of the problem. Such recognition acknowledges that an array of intricate policy and intellectual efforts as well as dedication to implementation are essential to fighting poverty.

However, even if more funding is the crux of the problem, and the World Bank is pivotal to mobilizing and channeling it, a host of issues arise about the nature of that financing, especially the terms on which it is provided to poorer countries. The most straightforward question turns around whether such financing should come in the form of loans—as envisaged for IBRD from its creation—or grants, which might attach few if any financial or policy strings. This question deeply engages the World Bank and other participants in development finance, not just bilateral aid donors, but also the regional development banks and export credit agencies.

The debt crises and economic turbulence that shook many developing countries and the global financial system in the 1980s and 1990s put fundamental questions about debt financing squarely on the public policy agenda. The World Bank's modus operandi clearly involves lending, largely on commercial terms, because that is seen as encouraging private lending and investment to promote development, and disciplined investment choices (governments are seen as more likely to spend wisely when they know the money has to be repaid). However, as world economic conditions and the abysmal economic performance of several countries shook confidence in lending portfolios, questions arose as to how to handle the debt of poor countries, which many could obviously not repay. Questions also arose as to whether lending was appropriate at all, given the fragile prospects of many poor nations and their pressing need to spend scarce funds on social programs.

The World Bank has been and remains in the eye of the hurricane for the international response to poor country debt. This hurricane has followed a protracted and convoluted path. Early in its history, the Bank established the principle that repayment of debt was a sacrosanct obligation, and through its policies and procedures insisted that countries give priority to servicing their debt. For decades the simple answer to debt troubles was that the World Bank did not reschedule, and if countries delayed their payments new lending was stopped, and disbursements to projects were suspended.

However, as shock after economic shock shook countries in different regions, the Bank responded with economic policy reforms designed to address the problems that made debt unmanageable in the first place. Next came new lending—special debt packages, including the Brady bonds for Mexico—that enabled governments to climb out of crisis and service their external debts, including those from the World Bank and the International Monetary Fund (IMF). Then, as debt burdens mounted even further, countries borrowing International Bank for Reconstruction and Development (IBRD) funds gained access to funding on easier terms, including from IDA. Negotiated settlements addressed the knotty legacy of unpayable commercial bank debt (participants were known collectively as the London Club, though a number of committees addressed debt rescheduling country by country). Bilateral debts—those made directly from richer to poorer nations—were subject to a highly disciplined if unstructured process of country-by-country negotiations through the Paris Club, managed by the French treasury.

But despite this onion peel of approaches unfolding in country after country, it became increasingly apparent to people in government treasuries, the World Bank, and civil society that many countries simply could not service their debts, and that heavy debt burdens were sapping their ability to engage in development programs. A lively debate about debt policies produced special measures, including the Fifth Dimension program, which financed service payments on IBRD debt for countries no longer eligible for such loans, buyback of debt from commercial banks, and higher allocations of IDA credits to needy countries. This debate also spurred a global mobilization that culminated in the Jubilee 2000 movement, which called for sharp reductions in debt and, in appropriate cases, cancellation and forgiveness.

The remarkable pincer effect resulting from vehement public protests, creative policy initiatives, and extended negotiations led to far-reaching changes in international debt policies. A major breakthrough came in 1996 with approval of the Heavily Indebted Poor Countries (HIPC) initiative, the first comprehensive approach to reducing the external debt of the world's poorest and most heavily indebted countries. With the World Bank as a central player, HIPC explicitly sought to place debt relief within an overall framework of poverty reduction. This initiative was closely allied with the poverty reduction strategy process (PRSP) mechanism, which established a country-led and World Bank- and IMF-assisted process of strategic planning turning around poverty and resulting in debt relief (see Chapter 3). Countries that qualified for HIPC assistance were also eligible for IDA assistance, as well as the IMF's Poverty Reduction and Growth Facility. An HIPC Trust Fund administered by IDA and funded by donors, including the IBRD, helped relieve debt by offering development grants, purchasing and canceling IDA loans, and servicing IDA debt. From 1999 on, IDA assumed responsibility for providing debt relief, reimbursed by the HIPC Trust Fund to the extent that funds are available. Debate on pragmatic modifications to the system now in place continues. Table 7.1 shows the status of the countries whose debts have been relieved through the HIPC initiative.

However, the often traumatic experience surrounding successive negotiations, as special measures failed to produce clear results in terms of tangible progress in poor countries, led many to question whether lending on even the most concessional terms, especially for the poorest countries, was appropriate. This question—concerning when, whether, and how much assistance poor countries should receive as grants rather than loans—opens a can of worms. First and most obviously, grants prevent banks from functioning as banks, as they

Table 7.1 Highly indebted poor countries (41 countries) (as of October 2007)

Completion point (22 countries)	Decision point (10 countries)	Pre-decision point (9 countries)
Benin	Afghanistan	Comoros
Bolivia	Burundi	Côte d'Ivoire
Burkina Faso	Central African	Eritrea
Cameroon	Republic	Kyrgyz Republic
Ethiopia	Chad	Liberia
Ghana	Democratic Republic of	Nepal
Guyana	Congo	Somalia
Honduras	Republic of Congo	Sudan
Madagascar	The Gambia	Togo
Malawi	Guinea	
Mali	Guinea-Bissau	
Mauritania	Haiti	
Mozambique		
Nicaragua		
Níger		
Rwanda		
São Tomé Príncipe		
Senegal		
Sierra Leone		
Tanzania		
Uganda		
Zambia		

Note:
The HIPC initiative currently identifies 41 countries, most of them in Sub-Saharan Africa, as potentially eligible to receive debt relief.

receive no repayments, so governments or other sources need to provide greater and continued funding. Second, grants do not necessarily entail the same kinds of mutual obligations that lending does.

These issues came to the fore, where they remain, in negotiations to replenish IDA—the single largest source for financing the global commitment to ending poverty. The twelfth and thirteenth replenishments of IDA (see Table 2.1) provided a significant proportion of funding for the poorest countries, especially for HIV/AIDS programs and reconstruction after armed conflict, as grants. Negotiations for the fifteenth replenishment of IDA kicked off in early 2007, with every expectation that difficult discussions on amounts, terms, and priorities for lending lay ahead given the upsurge in bilateral development aid, the controversies surrounding the Bank's president, Paul Wolfowitz, and the variety of other options, including private sector development, emerging for client and donor countries alike.

The World Bank has expanded its grant programs over the years, now overseen through its Development Grants Facility, established in 1997 to ensure strategic orientation and coordination of grant activities. Funding for these grants comes from profits on lending, as well as through trust funds provided by other agencies and administered by the Bank. The array of Development Grants Facility (DGF) activities includes large and proven programs like the Consultative Group on International Agricultural Research and the West African river blindness program, as well as programs that are explicitly catalytic and experimental, such as efforts to develop community foundations that mobilize local resources for development purposes (see Chapter 4).

The costs of doing business present a further set of financial challenges. The World Bank is an expensive operation—its administrative budget was approaching $2 billion in 2007—and its budget has come under increasingly close scrutiny for several decades. Financial controls occur through changes (i.e., reductions) in staffing levels, efforts to ensure careful planning and to expand partnerships (though in practice the cost savings when several partners are involved can be illusory), and greater hiring of staff working in countries (generally at lower cost). The balance between prudent use of funds and the capacity to undertake ever more complex tasks produces constant debate. While many are common to any large institution, the broad scope of the World Bank's work, and the extraordinary demands and high stakes entailed in even fairly technical tasks—such as assessing a country's public expenditures—make budget stewardship particularly difficult.

Priorities and tensions: global or regional?

Another set of challenges turns around the balance among the World Bank's many roles. The tension between two important currents, in particular, plays out daily: demands that the Bank respond to the needs, priorities, and circumstances of the countries that are its primary "clients," versus its *raison d'être* and mandate as a global institution with a global agenda. The push and pull between those poles is constant and often creative, forcing the institution to confront and reconcile its global perspective with the realities of engaging in individual countries. While the Bank's recent focus on grounding operations within each country, and basing country directors there, makes eminent sense, over time the World Bank clearly must act as a World Bank, giving high priority to encouraging cross-country sharing of experience, and pursuing global agendas more than the agendas of individual countries. A contemporary issue that links the two is remittance flows.

A related and knotty set of issues arises from the "vertical" programs (for example, global campaigns on a particular health problem or for universal primary education) that the World Bank has been asked to lead—many of which come with dedicated financing—and its leadership role for complex programs that arise from the broad global experience with development (as opposed to in response to country requests). Such experience includes the vital importance of educating girls; the Education for All initiative, both of which are transnational with common global objectives; various disease initiatives, and other programs that work from global targets, some tied explicitly to the MDG framework; and from there to programs in individual countries, rather than the reverse. These efforts prompt concern that a global apparatus will dilute the focus on individual countries, and lead to a proliferation of programs rather than a comprehensive and harmonized framework.

These debates are normal fare for international institutions like the World Bank to some extent, but beneath the discussions lie very different notions of how to spur change in a globalized world. Grounding analysis and action in the realities of individual countries makes eminent sense, because that is where development actually occurs. However, the roster of issues that must be addressed internationally is large and growing, including migration, global warming, remittance flows, terrorist financing, and banking and investment standards.[4]

Doing business

Both the staff and the governors of the World Bank constantly debate the institution's priorities and different paths to achieving them. These subjects include the appropriate balance between "hard" sectors such as infrastructure, and "softer" sectors, especially investments in human capabilities. One contemporary pull, reminiscent of the World Bank's early days, is toward more emphasis on the productive apparatus seen as key to unleashing investment and jobs: transport, power, and water. The Bank is seen as qualified by experience to mobilize the public-private partnerships needed to support such infrastructure investments, and able to ensure adherence to global environmental and social standards and clean financial management.

This camp regards the Bank as venturing too far into substantial investments in social sectors, including education, health, and community development. Yet evidence mounts daily that such investments in human capacity and in the poorest people (hence rural development) are vital to economic development. Agriculture was a high priority in the 1970s, for example, but problems with projects in that sector dampened the Bank's enthusiasm for such investments, particularly in Africa. However, the importance of agriculture to developing economies and communities, especially the rural poor, has recently brought a revival of interest. The real issue is not whether one or the other investment pole will dominate but the balance between them—both within countries and at the global level. Linking different sectors and integrating development are vitally important, and the World Bank, with its broad perspective and extensive experience, should clearly excel at this.

Efforts to strike the best balance among specific projects with finite, carefully defined objectives, technical assistance, and capacity building; operations with a sectoral focus; and support for national and subnational policy programs also present continuing challenges. Experience shows that a combination of these instruments works best, especially when programs actively engage development partners and add up to a coherent and harmonized picture. The mix can and should vary by country, and will continue to evolve over time.

The World Bank looks to an extraordinary body of experience and detailed assessments to determine the optimal mix, of which *Assessing Aid: What Works and What Doesn't* is an excellent example.[5] That report highlights one of the most fundamental if hardly surprising conclusions from development experience: that investments and development succeed where policy and governance environments are sound.

More broadly, the complex development field today is replete with wisdom, new initiatives, fads, and reminders of core understandings. Wise efforts include a new emphasis on empowering communities, requiring gender analysis to make more explicit the consequences of policies and programs for women and men, and relying on structured consultations to open the door to new voices. There is also a healthy recognition among development practitioners that quality matters, but that it depends on the specific situation. Quality standards for road construction may well be similar in Samoa and Argentina, for example, but school curricula should look very different, despite common threads underlying educational success in very different places. The danger is that a focus on the "issue of the day" can obscure the complex problems and common-sense choices that make up the development challenge. It is striking that most veterans of the development process, wherever they have worked, open discussions of what they have learned by emphasizing how complex the development process is, how many surprises it continually brings, and the vital importance of humility.

An important set of reflections concerns the World Bank's approach to three groups of countries on different parts of the development spectrum. The first are middle-income countries, whose happy contemporary reality is that they can secure financing for development programs from various sources including private investors. Some suggest that the World Bank gracefully withdraw from those countries and refocus its energies on poorer countries. However, there are strong reasons, notably the poverty issues plaguing even middle-income countries and the potential for the Bank to learn from successful country experience, for the Bank to continue operating in the middle-income group, with three provisos.

First, the Bank needs to bring excellent skills and a capacity for prompt and efficient response to bear when it is up against competition (it should always meet those tests of excellence, of course). Second, it needs to balance skillfully its mandate to uphold high standards, especially in the environmental and social arenas, with their suitability for each country. While the oft-expressed fear that high standards will scare away borrowers who have other options is oversimplified—many borrowers look to the Bank to help them raise standards and gain a reputation for excellence—over-designed and boilerplate approaches, and the resulting costs and delays, will plainly dampen enthusiasm for working with the World Bank.

Third, linking demanding new programs in middle-income countries to cross-country sharing of early experiences and best practices is particularly important. An example is conditional cash-transfer programs in Mexico and Brazil, which rely on direct financial support to encourage families to keep children in school and take them to clinics.[6]

A second important group of countries are those that are poorly governed and failing, termed by the World Bank Low Income Countries Under Stress (LICUS) or, more recently, fragile states. These weak, sometimes failing states present a major strategic challenge because they frustrate global efforts to fight poverty, exacerbate instability, and fuel popular anger about injustice. These nations also present special frustrations because they tend to defy most classic approaches to development: investments and projects rarely work, advice is often not heeded, armed conflict destroys even what is there, and a vicious circle spins round and round. Better approaches that build capacity even in fragile and uncertain situations, support education and health, and position the World Bank and other actors to move boldly and quickly when a promising change in direction occurs are vital.

Africa is the third and most important challenge, and few doubt that it presents the most critical test for development today. The

World Bank has been and remains a particularly important partner in Africa, offering a vast array of programs involving all countries on the continent. The sobering lessons of past failures are reflected in today's focus on reforming economic policy, continually engaging African partners, adapting programs to the specific realities of each country, and the central issue of good governance. However often the priority of Africa is affirmed, it is not enough, but the real challenge is to translate rhetorical commitment and careful plans (like the UK Commission on Africa) into reality. Figure 7.1 illustrates the frustration of the continuing challenge of keeping Africa at the top of the global agenda.

Ideas or cash? The knowledge Bank

While many view the World Bank primarily through a financing lens, its intellectual work is arguably at least as important. A host of issues turn on how the institution can best handle its knowledge role.

The World Bank as knowledge bank involves three strands of ideas. First, it has accumulated extraordinary experience and wisdom and, with a boost from information technology, can and should put this goldmine to growing use. Second, information technology is a critical ally for an institution with an explicitly global mandate. The Bank

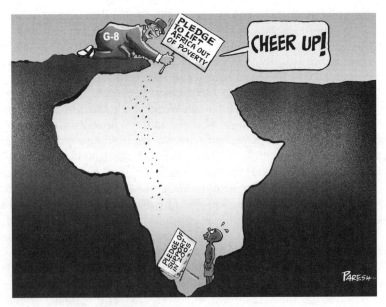

Figure 7.1 Illustrating priority to Africa.

should focus on supporting the networks that can link communities across the world, paying special attention to meeting the needs of those who have the least access to information.

Third, the World Bank faces the special challenges inherent for so-called knowledge institutions: a dynamic, feisty institution composed of particularly well-educated, intelligent people, many highly committed (though naturally with its share of those most interested in the success and comfort of their own careers). These challenges reflect the fact that the Bank works all over the world, and the multidisciplinary and multisectoral composition of its staff and work. Strong leadership within a framework of respect for ideas and difference, decentralization to allow local initiative wherever possible, subtle but clear incentives for both excellence and flexibility, and a human face are vital if the World Bank is to maximize its enormous potential for good in the twenty-first century.

Summary

The World Bank stands at a crossroads, facing a wide range of strategic challenges and choices. They will affect how central a player the future World Bank will be in the architecture of global development institutions, how large its mandate, portfolio and thus staff will be, how globally it will operate, notably how significant its role will be in middle-income countries and in the fragile states. Will the future Bank be near the center of the development solar system, or will its influence and activities decline in the face of the growing complexity and competitiveness of the international development system? The debate reflects both realities and perceptions, and how the Bank responds will materially affect its future.

Among the many issues the Bank faces, seven stand out: (a) the size and scope of the Bank's mandate, thus whether a "selectivity" or a "comprehensive" framework dominate; (b) how much money the Bank is able to mobilize to support the priorities it advocates, notably through replenishments of IDA; (c) how the international community deals with debates on debts versus loans and thus whether the Bank's lending mandate has a future and whether it has sufficient resources to support a sustainable grant program; (d) the balance between country focus and global and "global public goods" priorities and focus; if the latter, new instruments and financing mechanisms will be essential; (e) specific measures to address the distracted interest of newly courted middle-income countries which no longer need the Bank's financial support and thus must be attracted by its effectiveness and service, and new instruments and approaches allowing it to operate more effectively in fragile states; (f) how effectively the Bank addresses the challenges that go with being a contemporary knowledge institution, including a highly educated and feisty staff and management of technology; and (g) remaining relevant and competitive in terms of costs of doing business and focus on issues (whether infrastructure, education, or environment) that matter most to member countries.

8 Conclusion

An ideal for the World Bank

The World Bank of 2007 faces challenges more numerous and more complex, that cut deeper than any that have emerged in its earlier history. Yet beneath the debates lies a profound quest: for the institution, for its member nations, and its staff to achieve the heroic ideal and tangible goal of a "world free of poverty." This goal—to fulfill the essential needs of the world's poorest two billion people by ensuring access to health, education, food, shelter, jobs, and, above all, the opportunity to develop their potential—has changed from a dim ideal held by a few to a strong moral compass that guides, in ways that are increasingly effective, global institutions, including prominently the World Bank. The global community needs to be held to their promises and constantly encouraged in this mission. It is not enough, either, for the World Bank to direct people to posters showing progress on the Millennium Development Goals (MDGs) or to the marble slogan declaring its "dream of a world free of poverty"; some cynics note with irony that the words are firmly affixed to the wall, as if this is always to remain a dream. We cannot let this be the case.

The challenge goes deeper still because meeting basic human needs is not enough (though they need constant focus lest they be lost in more time-pressing goals). As part of the UN system, the World Bank also embraces the challenges involved in building a global community that is just and equitable, that encourages and protects diverse cultures and paths, and that translates human-rights ideals into tangible protection for individuals and communities, struggling as it strives towards these ideals to represent both the views of staff and the mandate of donor and client countries.

The World Bank occupies a somewhat uneasy place in what is loosely termed the global community. As a cooperative of nation-states—their powers exercised largely through their finance ministries, and reflecting the clear power structure that comes with relative economic strength—

the Bank meshes its governance with the ideals of a democratic community of nations with difficulty. However, the World Bank can play a creative and positive role in weaving together both the visionary and the pragmatic strands of global institutions.

The Bank is well positioned to appreciate the strengths and weaknesses of national governments, which continue—despite the rhetoric about globalization pushing aside the Westphalian state system—to play central roles in the lives of most citizens. Through many different lenses, but especially the many very earth-bound operations of the World Bank and International Finance Corporation (IFC), the Bank is also closely allied with private business and the international financial markets, which are an increasingly powerful global force. The Bank long kept civil society at arms' length, but today engages actively with myriad nongovernmental organizations all over the world. And the Bank has overlapping interests and at least some engagement with most if not all the central organizations and specialized agencies within the UN system.

The World Bank's undemocratic governance structure is likely to come under growing pressure. While major reforms in the Bank's ownership structure and weighted voting system seem unlikely, its broader accountability and governance systems are in fact being transformed by the far greater openness of the contemporary era; few of its actions escape scrutiny today. A complex accountability framework, combined with the World Bank's engagement in multiple worlds, poses the ironic threat that it can lead to a stifling of initiative and even paralysis. That is a real and present risk. If, however, the Bank and its governors and leaders can respond positively and creatively to the accountability challenge, the World Bank could bring an extraordinarily effective voice to global debates, and a practical hand to the enormous tasks that lie ahead in fighting poverty and advancing social justice.

The development community today is a far cry from the small, well-defined group of institutions working in the field in the early 1950s, and even into the 1970s. Countless entities with mandates related to development, poverty, and equity now work in poor countries, and keeping track of their activities has become virtually impossible. While this proliferation encourages initiative, engagement, and creativity, it is bewildering and burdensome for many of the people the institutions are designed to serve, especially leaders and managers in developing countries. Many consider the system overall and many of its parts seriously broken, because of overlapping and contradictory efforts and the significant inefficiencies that result.

The good news is that harmonization and partnership are watchwords of the day, and serious efforts to achieve both are under way. Aid harmonization is very much a work in progress, and an area where the World Bank's unique position and experience lend itself particularly well to a leadership role. The Bank knows well the pitfalls of poorly tuned aid procedures, and the drawbacks of conflicting systems of procurement and accounts. It also understands the history and interests that gave rise to the different systems. The World Bank itself is not immune to going it alone and to dogmatism, which sometimes accentuate the problems. However, the pragmatic and powerful World Bank, when it is at the fore, can move mountains, and could help in the Herculean task ahead of ensuring decentralized decision-making and diverse creativity within a framework of defined common goals and honest and probing dialogue and action on contentious issues. The World Bank can achieve this through its own extensive experience with partnerships that engage virtually every type of institution working in development.

The many financial dimensions of the World Bank's work and role give it special strengths but also present difficult challenges. The Bank's privileged financial position is an undoubted strength: relative to many if not most other institutions working in development (with the possible exception of the Bill and Melinda Gates Foundation), the Bank has unparalleled financial capacity to translate ideas and plans into action. It has a long track record of mobilizing funds from richer governments and private financial markets. And it has practical contacts with the private sector, which has grown astronomically in importance: private net capital flows to the developing world rose from an estimated $85 billion in 1990 to nearly $650 billion in 2006.

Yet in some respects, the World Bank still operates on assumptions derived from the international financial system of bygone days—one that situated investments and projects within a national development plan with predictable results. The World Bank's large size and legendary complexity, including constraints linked to its intricate accountability system, are disadvantages if they delay response and stifle creativity and openness to new ideas. Many bold and creative ventures within the institution, however, are evolving alongside the rather chaotic, fast-paced world of international finance. With constant and pragmatic adaptation to changing realities, the World Bank can maximize its advantages and overcome its liabilities.

Politics is a fundamental part of poverty, and few global issues have as many or more complex political dimensions as poverty and equity. The World Bank has therefore long faced several conundrums. It must aim to be seen as fair, balanced, open to persuasion, and driven by evidence, if it is to gain the trust and respect it needs to succeed in its work at all levels. The prohibition against direct political involvement inherited from the original Bretton Woods discussions has often served the Bank well, allowing it to step back from the fray within individual countries. However, the question of what will become of the "p" word (politics)—traditionally barely mentionable in World Bank settings—is very much on the table. The Bank increasingly recognizes that political analysis is essential to understanding poverty, and that a solid appreciation of political forces is essential to designing effective programs to combat it.

Two special related challenges stand out. The first is how the World Bank can and should balance its carefully nurtured neutrality (leading to hesitation to engage overtly in a politicized fray) with its role as an advocate and voice for poor people, communities, and countries. Of course, the Bank's reputation for fairness has some tarnish, as many view the institution as deeply biased toward certain economic models, as elevating economics above other disciplines, and above all as dominated by the United States. However, the World Bank should be able to use wise stewardship to enhance its reputation for intellectual honesty and rigor, given the widespread respect even among tough critics for its technical work in many fields. The cause of poverty and the world's poor communities would be poorly served if the World Bank were to stand aside from highly politicized debates about trade reform, for example, as its field experience and analysis stand to shed light on many dimensions of this complex and vital problem, or global warming, where similar arguments apply. The solution may lie in a more forthright recognition of the tension among these roles, and an active willingness to entertain conflicting evidence and views at every stage.

Governance also has entered the World Bank lexicon. Governance has very different connotations in differing settings, and is sometimes used essentially as a code word for corruption. Paul Wolfowitz's two-year tenure as World Bank president (2005–7) shone a controversial spotlight on that topic. The erratic and untransparent application of his principles across countries and the spectacle of his public stance as a judge of countries' anti-corruption performance conflicting with his personal ethics set back thoughtful debate about the topic. Nonetheless, from the fray and extensive consultations a far more coherent strategy for governance reform including the optimal roles that the World Bank can play have emerged.

Three sensible conclusions have emerged that suggest paths to action in this arena. The first is that the World Bank's longstanding efforts to strengthen systems designed to prevent corruption—largely through technical analysis, reforms of accountability systems and specific project safeguards—were necessary but far from sufficient. Corruption deserves to be discussed openly and continuously, and development programs need to be designed—overall and in their individual components—to assure both beneficiaries and funders that resources will be well spent. This effort is morally important, as stealing and waste are wrong in virtually all settings; it is important for effectively implementing programs of all sorts; and it is a political imperative in building trust. Second, corruption is neither an incurable nor a temporary disease. There are good mechanisms for combating it, and these can and should be employed. And third, good governance is not synonymous with anti-corruption; the latter is a small part of the broader need for effective, reliable, and trusted institutions to guide development.

The World Bank has set itself a bold and essential challenge: to fight poverty with passion and professionalism. The professionalism goes largely without saying, but it hints at the institution's great pride in the rigor of its analysis and its dedication to marshaling the best solutions to problems in today's world. The passion is somewhat harder to define, but manifests above all as commitment to and concern about the work to be done. It is often seen in late-night work and discussion, a dogged determination to solve problems, and caring advocacy. The challenge is to ensure that individual and institutional passions are manifested in development results, the fruits of which people outside of governments can recognize.

Because the World Bank is such a complex and diverse organization, the commitment to fighting poverty is both subtle and deep. Most staff members appreciate well that fighting poverty is a difficult task that requires inputs from people in many fields, including economists, educators, microcredit specialists, engineers, doctors, and sociologists. It calls for creative partnerships linking multilateral institutions, private entrepreneurs, government leaders and administrators, civic activists, and academics. It needs more and better-used resources. And it requires a cooperative spirit that recognizes powerful common ground in concern about global poverty, but also respects and appreciates different approaches and the need to find better ways for development partners to work separately and together toward a shared goal.

Appendix

An ABC for understanding and working with the World Bank

The following counsel on working with the World Bank aims to provide some practical information and ideas for those interested in taking their knowledge of the World Bank a step further.

Acronyms and glossary The World Bank tends to use an extraordinary range of abbreviations in its work, and many words also have special connotations; it is in some respects a special language. Most units and reports provide their own glossary, many available on the web. A central source is the "disclosure glossary" at www.worldbank.org/

Board of Directors This full-time board of 24 executive directors— elected and appointed by the governors who represent the 185 member governments—is a unique and important feature of the World Bank's governance structure. When major crises or issues arise, the board is where the political wrangling and decisions take place.

Country information The country director and team have day-to-day leadership responsibility for virtually all World Bank activities in a country. A small unit at Washington headquarters—known as the anchor—liaises with each country office and fields questions about its activities. For most specific questions and issues, the best place to start is with the anchor or the country office. Most country offices have a public information center.

Decentralization Historically, the World Bank was highly centralized at its headquarters at 1818 H St. NW in Washington, DC. That is changing through a steady shift of both staff and decision-making responsibility to Bank offices in individual countries. Today more than 50 percent of the Bank's operational staff (though only about 40 percent of its total staff) are either posted from headquarters to work on-site in a country and/or hired locally.

Entry points The best places to find answers to queries about the World Bank are its country offices and its web site. For sectors in which the World Bank is heavily engaged, such as education or transport, a help desk for each reachable through the web site can guide questioners to the right person. Civil society institutions can interact with the civil society team in Washington, and with officers with civil society responsibilities posted to individual countries (their titles may vary).

Field offices The World Bank maintains about 120 offices in countries around the world, also called country offices. Most have a special focus on providing information.

Governors The Bank's governors—usually ministers of finance or planning appointed by member countries—make major decisions on membership and financial essentials. Governors meet at the pivotal annual meeting, held for two consecutive years in Washington and for one subsequent year in another city, rotating by region. These meetings attract many parallel activities, some run by the Bank and some hosted by other entities, including private banks and think tanks. The Development Committee which is an oversight body linking the International Monetary Fund (IMF) and World Bank meets in Washington, normally in May, with associated events such as meetings of the finance ministers of key countries. The Spring Meetings are smaller but in some respects are coming to rival the Bank's annual meeting in complexity and ancillary events.

Highly Indebted Poor Country (HIPC) initiative The HIPC is the framework for the carefully negotiated arrangements for relief of poor country debt A wide range of instruments and vocabulary go with it including the poverty reduction strategy process (PRSP) and specific types of lending instruments for which countries are eligible once they have passed HIPC "decision points."

International Finance Corporation The private sector arm of the World Bank Group, can lend directly to companies and take equity. This is the place to start for private-sector issues. The International Finance Corporation (IFC) has its own web site (www.ifc.org), ethos, country office structure, and policies.

Jobs Numerous applications and strict ceilings on hiring make jobs at the World Bank hard to come by. The Bank employs many consultants, selected because they have expertise that the Bank needs, or to cover gaps during peak periods. The Junior Professional Associate program is worth investigating if someone is under 29 and wants a two-year fixed-term experience, but the pool of applicants is large. The Bank actively recruits people mostly for specific positions and expertise.

Knowledge product   This term refers to a study or report; Analytic and Advisory Activities (AAA) means the same thing. Knowledge management usually refers to web-based systems that disseminate or share information.

Language   The World Bank opted early on for English as its official language, and it is still the lingua franca. However, many documents are translated into other languages, and the Bank operates in the language of individual countries whenever possible.

Monthly Operational Summary (MOS)   The MOS reports on the status of each lending operation being prepared for Bank financing, from its inception through signed agreements between the Bank and an individual country.

Numbers   Bank data are a treasure trove of information, and a respected core function of the institution. Data are increasingly available through the Bank's web site, with printed publications also available.

Organization   The Bank's president, managing director, and vice presidents are officers with clear, identifiable responsibilities. However, the titles of other positions can be confusing. The most difficult parts of the organization to penetrate are the networks and sector departments, which have a large array of titles within a matrix structure that tends to vary by region and leadership style. Team leaders—often termed task team leaders or TTLs—are the line staff who make many decisions and do most of the Bank's day-to-day work.

Procurement   The Bank has developed processes for purchasing goods and services that sometimes takes procurement to the level of art. Procurement procedures—whether for megaprojects, consulting services, or small tasks—are extensive, particular, and well worth studying.

Quality Assurance Group (QAG)   The QAG is a relatively new Bank team that randomly or by intent reviews operations at the time of approval, to provide practical and timely advice and oversight. Being QAGd is a source of considerable concern to those involved, akin to a final exam.

Reports and disclosure   The Bank is steadily moving information from behind closed doors into the public domain, particularly after reports are finalized and loans approved. Public information centers (PICs) in each country are a source of information. Continuing external pressure for more disclosure now focuses on the deliberations of the Executive Board, earlier drafts of documents, and reports on assessment of project implementation.

Safeguard policies   The Bank has approved so many policies that its own employees had real difficulty in following them all. Thus in 1998 the Bank designated a priority group of seven environmental policies and three social and cultural policies as "safeguard" policies, which are subject to elaborate oversight and reporting.

The World Bank Group   This refers to the major distinct organizations created in succession but managed as a whole (IBRD, IDA, IFC, MIGA, ICSID) and headquartered at 1818 H St. NW.

Tranche release   Most quick-disbursing policy-based loans and credits are divided into two or more parts, termed tranches. Meeting conditions that will permit the Bank to disburse a tranche of a loan is thus a pivotal activity for governments, staff and board.

UN Development Programme (UNDP)   UNDP is the key Bank partner within the United Nations (UN) system. It nominally coordinates all the activities of UN agencies in individual countries— sometimes playing this role superbly, sometimes less effectively. UNDP and the World Bank are close partners and sometime rivals, as they sometimes bump up against each other in their technical assistance roles. Practical arrangements for joint work vary widely by country.

Viewpoint   The Bank periodically publishes a collection of short working papers on a specific topic. The goal is to disseminate policy innovations and best practices, and to encourage private-sector and market-based solutions to development challenges.

Web site   The Bank invests many resources in its web site (www. worldbank.org), but it can be a challenge to navigate because it is huge and "message focused"—that is, it offers information the Bank thinks you want to know. Keep trying; there is gold there. Growing amounts of information on the Bank's programs and analysis are available on dedicated web sites.

X   Normally refers to exports. Promoting export growth has been a key and controversial element of Bank economic advice.

Young Professionals (YP)   YP is the competitive annual program for a small group of highly qualified development professionals under 33 years of age.

Robert Zoellick   President of the World Bank from July 2007, thus a first contact point for major issues: write to 1818 H St. NW, Washington DC 20433.

Notes

Foreword

1 See Elizabeth A. Mandeville and Craig N. Murphy, *The United Nations Development Programme* (London: Routledge, forthcoming 2008).
2 John Maynard Keynes, *The Economic Consequences of the Peace* (London: Macmillan, 1920) and *A Revision of the Treaty* (London: Macmillan, 1922); see also his *General Theory of Employment, Interest and Money* (London: Macmillan, 1936).
3 See, for example, Devesh Kapur, John P. Lewis, and Richard Webb, *The World Bank: Its First Half Century* (Washington, DC: Brookings, 1997).
4 See James Vreeland, *The International Monetary Fund: Politics of Conditional Lending* (London: Routledge, 2007); and Bernard M. Hoekman and Petros C. Mavroidis, *The World Trade Organization: Law, Economics and Politics* (London: Routledge, 2007).
5 William Easterly, *The Elusive Quest for Growth* (Cambridge, MA: MIT Press, 2001).

Introduction

1 See the Global Institutions series book on the IMF: James Vreeland, *The International Monetary Fund: Politics of Conditional Lending* (London: Routledge, 2007).
2 This term was coined by Denis Goulet in 1980, in an article published in *World Development* (Denis Goulet, "Development Experts: the One-Eyed Giants," *World Development* 8, no. 7–8 (1980): 481–89); the label has stuck.

1 "In the catbird's seat"

1 There is a vast literature on development, especially development economics; among the most influential thinkers are John Maynard Keynes, seminal economic thinker who was directly involved in the design of the IMF and World Bank, Walt Rostow, who, from the 1950s, combined a focus on the role of capital with a projected path of development that progressed in a linear manner, Nobel prize winner Sir Arthur Lewis, who articulated theoretical concepts of a divided world but also brought pragmatic dimensions into the picture, Simon Kuznets, also a Nobel laureate,

known among many other contributions for the rigor he brought to econo-
metric tools in analyzing economic trends, Albert Hirschman, who explored
the complex minefields of development experience with an unerring eye for its
complexities and lessons that might be learned, Gunnar Myrdal, who inter
alia injected social policy thinking and challenges into the development arena,
Paul Streeten, whose contributions included linking development more explicitly with trade, Raul Prebisch, one of many representatives of rethinking
development with the political lens of north south politics, Jomo KS, Malay-
sian economist who brings radical perspectives effectively into mainstream
discussions, Paul Krugman, whose work has also focused on development
and trade, and Amartya Sen, whose vast writings cover most issues but who
is perhaps best known for his insightful perspectives on human rights, development, and democracy. Some especially pertinent books include Albert
Hirschman, *The Passions and the Interests: Political Arguments for Capit-
alism before its Triumph* (Princeton: Princeton University Press, 1997, 20th
edition), Robert L. Tignor, *W. Arthur Lewis and the Birth of Development
Economics* (Princeton: Princeton University Press, 2005), Dwight H. Perkins,
Steven Radelet, and David L. Lindauer, *Economics of Development* (New
York: W. W. Norton, 2006), Robert H. Bates, *Prosperity and Violence: The
Political Economy of Development* (New York: W. W. Norton, 2001), and
Amartya Sen, *Development as Freedom* (New York: Anchor Books, 2000).

2 International financial institutions (sometimes termed IFIs) refers to institutions primarily concerned with international finance, including the IMF,
the World Bank, the regional development banks (see Chapter 4), export
credit agencies, and a range of other development institutions operating at
regional and global levels.

3 A series of particularly influential studies led by Deepa Narayan of the
World Bank under the broad heading of "Voices of the Poor" surveyed
poor communities across the world and documented different dimensions
of poverty and brought the voices of poor people into development dis-
course in an effective way; see Deepa Narayan, Raj Patel, Kai Schafft,
Anne Rademacher and Sarah Koch-Schulte, *Voices of the Poor: Can
Anyone Hear Us?* (New York: Published for the World Bank, Oxford
University Press, 2000), Deepa Narayan, Robert Chambers, Meera Kaul
Shah, and Patti Petesch, *Voices of the Poor: Crying Out for Change* (New
York: Published for the World Bank, Oxford University Press, 2000), and
Deepa Narayan and Patti Petesch, *Voices of the Poor: From Many Lands*
(New York: Published for the World Bank, Oxford University Press, 2002).

4 For an account of how the Jubilee mobilization changed the tenor and
content of global debates about debt and poverty see Chapter 3 in
Katherine Marshall and Lucy Keough, eds., *Mind, Heart and Soul in the
Fight against Poverty* (Washington, DC: the World Bank, 2004).

5 The UN Commission on Human Security, led by Sadako Ogata and
Amartya Sen, reported in May, 2003. Their report is available at www.
humansecurity-chs.org/finalreport/

6 Compassion International. See interview with Doug Bassett, http://berkley
center.georgetown.edu/BL%20FBO%20Bassett%20Interview%204%205.doc

7 www.un.org/millenniumgoals/

8 Based on the Millennium Declaration signed by World Leaders at the
United Nations, September 2000; www.un.org/millenniumgoals/goals.html

2 How the World Bank has evolved in response to global events

1 Several books describe the creation and early years of the World Bank, but the most comprehensive is the volume created for its twenty-fifth anniversary. See Edward S. Mason and Robert E. Asher, *The World Bank since Bretton Woods* (Washington, DC: Brookings Institution, 1973).

2 IBRD articles of agreement (as amended effective February 16, 1989), Article IV, section 10.

3 Mason and Asher, *The World Bank since Bretton Woods*, 35.

4 With the growing strength of the European Union, some suggest moving Bank headquarters to Europe, but this seems more like a dream or a venting of frustration than a likely prospect.

5 The articles also state: "The President shall cease to hold office when the Executive Directors so decide."

6 The World Bank has had several capital increases over the years and modifications in financial architecture which are not treated here in detail.

7 Mason and Asher, *The World Bank since Bretton Woods,* 54.

8 Mason and Asher, *The World Bank since Bretton Woods,* 58.

9 Mason and Asher, *The World Bank since Bretton* Woods, 380.

10 McNamara's speeches are still well worth reading; Robert S. McNamara, *The McNamara Years at the World Bank: Major Policy Addresses of Robert S. McNamara, 1968–1981* (Baltimore: The Johns Hopkins Press, 1981).

11 See for example the 2001 joint review on Strengthening IMF World Bank Collaboration on Country Programs and Conditionality, available at http://siteresources.worldbank.org/PROJECTS/Resources/imf-wb-conditionality08-22-01.pdf

12 See, notably, Joseph Stiglitz, *Globalization and its Discontents* (New York: W. W. Norton and Company, 2003).

13 China, through its government then located on mainland China, was one of the original Bretton Woods 44 institutions. After 1949, it was the government based in Taiwan that was the active World Bank member, and it was both a highly successful borrower and then lender. As negotiations proceeded for China's reentry, the position of Taiwan was a sore issue, intensively discussed. The issue remains sensitive to this day but the Republic of China retains special status including rights to participate in procurement for World Bank-financed operations.

14 For many years the Bank was far more active in the countries aligned with the West than in socialist countries, with some exceptions, which included the Bank's strong affinity for Tanzania. Several countries aligned with the Soviet bloc delayed membership, but by the 1990s all African countries had become members, and the Bank was active in all (except during periods of nonpayment of loans, as is the case with Sudan today).

15 Sebastian Mallaby's *The World's Banker: A Story of Failed States, Financial Crises, and the Wealth and Poverty of Nations* (New York: Penguin Press, 2004) provides a marvelous and detailed portrait of Wolfensohn and the Wolfensohn years at the World Bank.

16 See footnote 3, Chapter 1 for a full citation of Narayan *et al.*, op. cit.

17 For an excellent account of how environment came to the Bank and how the Bank came to the environment, see Robert Wade, "Greening the Bank: the Struggle over the Environment, 1970–95," in *The World Bank: Its First Half Century, Volume II: Perspectives,* ed. Devesh Kapur, John P. Lewis

and Richard Webb (Washington, DC: The Brookings Institution Press, 1997).

18 See, for example, Robert Picciotto and Michael Clarke, *Global Development and Human Security* (London: Transaction Publishers, 2007).

3 Nuts and bolts

1 This chapter should be read as complementary to and not a substitute for a *Guide to the World Bank* (Washington, DC: World Bank, 2007), which offers a wealth of explanations and data. With sufficient resourceful effort, the Bank's web site (www.worldbank.org) also usually yields answers to specific questions about policies and practices.

2 Utania is a fictional country (as are other places and situations in this case), a composite of different countries from several continents.

3 This picture of the nature and impact of differing perspectives is elaborated in the author's "Making Sense of Development Debates," which portrays 10 views expressed during a fictional aid coordination meeting. The working paper, prepared for the Harvard Institute for International Development (Development Discussion Paper 629, March 1998), is available at: www.ksg.harvard.edu/cid/hiid/629.pdf

4 IDA eligibility is determined by country, not the specific circumstances that a project is designed to address. Whether a specific operation received IDA or IBRD terms is thus rarely open to negotiation. Because of the large gap between IDA and IBRD terms, this gap often seems troublesome and rather rigid. For several years, a "third window" provided funds at intermediary terms (midway between IBRD and IDA), but the facility was considered too cumbersome and was not renewed. The purpose of blending terms is normally achieved through the IBRD IDA mix or, in some rare but important circumstances, by bilateral governments providing specific subsidies to IBRD terms; the most important case is China where the UK inter alia has funded the interest rate differential for some social sector operations.

5 See the World Bank web site for the Uganda and Tanzania JAS, and for a presentation on new features of these exercises. http://web.worldbank.org/WBSITE/EXTERNAL/COUNTRIES/AFRICAEXT/UGANDAEXTN/0, menuPK:374950~pagePK:141132~piPK:141105~theSitePK:374864,00.html for Uganda JAS, and http://info.worldbank.org/etools/docs/library/229631/CD4-JAS%20%28Melanie%20Marlett%29.ppt#274,3, Slide 3.

6 The PRSP page on the World Bank web site provides guidelines, a source book, up-to-date listings of PRSPs, and commentary and analysis.

7 The best-known review of portfolio performance was the Wapenhans report issued in July, 1992, which raised red flags about disappointing project performance and the trends that underlay it. Task Force Report on Portfolio Performance, "Effective Implementation: Key to Development Effectiveness," available at www.worldbank.org/html/opr/pmi/ta/ta000000.html

8 See www.gdnet.org/

9 See www.developmentgateway.org/

10 For the current issue and archives going back many years, see www.bankswirled.org/Frame.htm

11 web.worldbank.org/oed.about.html

12 The Inspection Panel web site includes information on all cases considered to date, as well as the workings of the Panel. Two books about the panel's work have been published. http://web.worldbank.org/WBSITE/EXTER-NAL/EXTINSPECTIONPANEL/0,menuPK:64132057~pagePK:64130364~piPK:64132056~theSitePK:380794,00.html

4 Development partnerships and the World Bank

1 A web site devoted to aid harmonization at www.aidharmonization.org/ has updates and rich information on various relevant initiatives.
2 www.oecd.org/document/18/0,2340,en_2649_3236398_35401554_1_1_1_1,00.html
3 www.aidharmonization.org/ah-st/ah-browser/index-abridged?master=master&rgn_cnt=gh
4 Personal communication with Simon Maxwell, ODI, July 2006.
5 Hilary Benn Speech to APGOOD, 14 March 2006.
6 World Bank: HIV/AIDS in the Caribbean Region: A Multi-Organization Review – Draft Final Report, 2005.
7 DAC survey on harmonization and alignment, 2006—available from ODI.
8 The OECD groups 30 member countries sharing a commitment to democratic government and the market economy. With active relationships with some 70 other countries and economies, NGOs and civil society, it has a global reach. Best known for its publications and its statistics, its work covers economic and social issues from macroeconomics, to trade, education, development and science and innovation. The Development Assistance Committee (DAC, www.oecd.org/dac) is the principal body through which the OECD deals with issues related to cooperation with developing countries.
9 IFC has its own web site: www.ifc.org. A lengthy history of IFC by Jonas Haralz appears on the IFC web site. See www.ifc.org/ifcext/50thanniversary.nsf/AttachmentsByTitle/Haralz_Full_Document/$FILE/Haralz_Full_Document_Edited.pdf. See also Bretton Woods Project 2000 review of the World Bank and the Private Sector: http://www.brettonwoodsproject.org/art-15925
10 www.ifc.org/ifcext/economics.nsf/Content/ic-wbes
11 See www.ifc.org/ifcext/equatorprinciples.nsf/AttachmentsByTitle/FactSheets/$FILE/EQUATOR+PRINCIPLES+FACT+SHEET.pdf
12 Search the GEF web site for project information and documents at www.gefonline.org
13 MIGA's web site is at www.miga.org
14 www.developmentgateway.org/
15 See www.world-links.org/
16 The author directs WFDD which is based at the Georgetown University Berkley Center for Religion, Peace and World Affairs, http://berkleycenter.georgetown.edu/
17 See www.cgiar.org/
18 Michael Specter, "What Money can Buy," *The New Yorker* (October 24, 2005): 56–71. Abstract available at www.newyorker.com/archive/2005/10/24/051024fa_fact_specter

5 Grounding in realities

1 See, for example, Lawrence Hinkle, "External Adjustment in the CFA Zone: Issues and Options," unpublished staff paper (Washington, DC: World Bank, August 1991), and Lawrence E. Hinkle and Peter Montiel, *Exchange Rate Misalignment: Concepts and Measurement for Developing Countries* (New York: Oxford University Press, 1999).
2 The Gambia story is told in greater detail in Katherine Marshall, *Vision and Relationships in the International Aid World: the Gambia-World Bank Kairaba Partnership Forum* (Cambridge, MA: Harvard Institute for International Development, 1997).
3 For an evaluation of the ASEM trust fund experience, see *ASEM Asian Financial Crisis Response Fund: Completion Review* (Washington, DC: The World Bank, May 2003), available at http://siteresources.worldbank.org/ASEM/Resources/asemcompletionreport-may2003.pdf
4 See Katherine Marshall and Olivier Butzbach, *New Social Policy Agendas for Europe and Asia* (Washington, DC: World Bank, 2002).
5 The IP's press release on its inspection is available at http://web.worldbank.org/WBSITE/EXTERNAL/EXTINSPECTIONPANEL/0,contentMDK:20227238~menuPK:64129469~pagePK:64129751~piPK:64128378~theSitePK:380794,00.html

6 The World Bank and its critics

1 Jonathan Fox and L. David Brown, *The Struggle for Accountability: the World Bank, NGOs, and Grassroots Movements* (Cambridge, MA: The MIT Press, 1998), and John D. Clark, *Worlds Apart: Civil Society and the Battle for Ethical Globalization* (Bloomfield, CT: Kumarian Press, 2003).
2 See www.50years.org/. Another web site with an equally blunt message was www.abolishthebank.org (though this has now mutated to a site on anarchist movements).
3 Examples, besides the well-known commentaries of William Easterly, are books by Josef Ritzen, *A Chance for the World Bank* (Anthem Press, 2005), and David Ellermann (forward by Albert O. Hirschman), *Helping People Help Themselves: From the World Bank to an Alternative Philosophy of Development Assistance (Evolving Values for a Capitalist World)* (Ann Arbor: University of Michigan Press, 2006).
4 I am indebted to Professor Bob Goudzwaard, Professor Emeritus of Economics and long tied to the World Council of Churches for his formulation of three Es to highlight concerns about the World Bank: empire, effects, and enigma.
5 See www.brettonwoodsproject.org/item.shtml?x=537848
6 Susan George and Fabrizio Sabeli, *Faith and Credit: The World Bank's Secular Empire* (Boulder, CO: Westview Press, 1994); William Easterly, *The Elusive Quest for Growth: Economists' Adventures and Misadventures in the Tropics* (Cambridge, MA: MIT Press, 2002); Catherine Caulfield, *Masters of Illusion: The World Bank and the Poverty of Nations* (New York: Henry Holt, 1996). Another hard-hitting critique is Jeffrey Hooke's *The Dinosaur Among Us: The World Bank and Its Path to Extinction* (Charleston, SC: Book Surge: 2007).

7 The report of the Meltzer commission is available at www.house.gov/jec/ imf/meltzer.htm

8 Robert Picciotto, "What Is Human Security?" Kings College, Cambridge, UK, available at www.gdnet.org/pdf2/gdn_library/annual_conferences/seventh_ annual_conference/icciotto_parallel_3_6.pdf

9 Jessica Einhorn, "The World Bank's Mission Creep," *Foreign Affairs* 80, no. 5 (September/October 2001): 22–35.

10 The report is available at http://siteresources.worldbank.org/DEC/Resources/ 84797—1164121166494/RESEARCH-EVALUATION-2006-Main-Report.pdf

11 The Development Committee is a forum of the World Bank and the International Monetary Fund that facilitates intergovernmental consensus-building on development issues. Known formally as the Joint Ministerial Committee of the Boards of Governors of the Bank and the Fund on the Transfer of Real Resources to Developing Countries, it was established in 1974 and advises the Boards of Governors of the Bank and the Fund on critical development issues and on the financial resources required to promote economic development in developing countries. Over the years, the Committee has interpreted this mandate to include trade and global environmental issues in addition to traditional development matters.

12 See chapter 3 in Katherine Marshall and Lucy Keough, eds., *Mind, Heart, and Soul in the Fight Against Poverty* (Washington, DC: World Bank, 2004): 35–45 for a discussion of the movement, and how it fought to bring about change in what was seen as an intractable problem.

7 Looking ahead

1 See Jeffrey Sachs, *The End of Poverty: Economic Possibilities for Our Time* (New York: Penguin, 2006). See also UN Millennium Project, *Overview: Investing in Development* (New York: Earthscan, 2005), a massive review of progress (or lack thereof) in achieving the MDGs, designed to bolster the effort and provide the first major benchmark on the way to 2015.

2 There are many examples of such calculations. OECD has a good overview. Both the UN and World Bank calculate and periodically reassess the costs of achieving the MDGs, for example at http://www.worldbank.org/ html/extdr/mdgassessment.pdf. Many calculations are made for sectors, for example health and education.

3 For more on the One campaign, see www.one.org/

4 Jean-François Rischard, former vice president of the World Bank, has written a fascinating book with the captivating title *High Noon* (New York: Basic Books, 2003), which defines 20 global problems, contends that we have only 20 years to solve them, and argues that new mechanisms outside the existing international architecture must be developed to address them.

5 The World Bank, *Assessing Aid: What Works and What Doesn't* (Washington, DC: the World Bank, 1998).

6 For a paper on this experience (part of a large and growing literature), see http://siteresources.worldbank.org/INTISPMA/Resources/Training-Events-and-Materials/PRMPR-CCT.pdf

Select bibliography

Paul Collier, *The Bottom Billion: Why the Poorest Countries are Failing and What Can Be Done About It* (Oxford: Oxford University Press, 2007). Superb and paradigm changing analysis of contemporary development issues.

David Ellermann, *Helping People Help Themselves: From the World Bank to an Alternative Philosophy of Development Assistance* (Ann Arbor: University of Michigan, 2006). Example of an economics-grounded critique of World Bank policies by a former Bank staff member.

Richard E. Feinberg, and contributors. *Between Two Worlds: The World Bank's Next Decade* (New Brunswick, NJ: Transaction Books, 1986). An example of a thoughtful review of development issues, including poverty, debt, and financing, by a think tank—in this case, the Overseas Development Council.

Devesh Kapur, John P. Lewis, and Richard Webb, *The World Bank: Its First Half-Century, Volume I: History; Volume II: Perspectives* (Washington, DC: Brookings Institution, 1997). Officially commissioned by the World Bank, this is an independent, extensive history of the Bank and major issues it faced.

Jochem Kraske, William H. Becker, William Diamond, and Louis Galambos, *Bankers with a Mission: The Presidents of the World Bank, 1946–91* (Washington, DC: World Bank, 1996).

Sebastian Mallaby, *The World's Banker: A Story of Failed States, Financial Crises, and the Wealth and Poverty of Nations* (New York: Penguin Press, 2004). A lively and insightful account of the World Bank focused on the Wolfensohn years.

Edward S. Mason and Robert E. Asher, *The World Bank since Bretton Woods: The Origins, Policies, Operations, and Impact of the International Bank for Reconstruction and Development and the Other Members of the World Bank Group* (Washington, DC: Brookings Institution, 1973). A comprehensive discussion of the Bank's first quarter-century, prepared independently but with World Bank support.

Robert Picciotto and Rachel Weaving, eds. *Impact of Rich Countries' Policies on Poor Countries: Towards a Level Playing Field in Development Cooperation* (New Brunswick, NJ: Transaction Publishers, 2004).

Josef Ritzen, *A Chance for the World Bank* (foreword by Joseph Stiglitz) (London: Anthem Press, 2005). Thoughtful discussion of twenty-first-century challenges by a former vice president for human development at the World Bank and Dutch political leader.

World Development Report (Washington, DC: World Bank). Published each year on a different topic, these are generally thorough and excellent documents.

Web sites

www.worldbank.org
www.ifc.org
www.miga.org
www.icsid.org
www.brettonwoodsproject.org/
www.cgd.org

Index

Boxed material is indicated by "b" after page numbers. Tables and diagrams are indicated by *italic* page numbers.

GLOBAL INSTITUTIONS SERIES

NEW TITLE
The World Trade Organization
Law, economics, and politics

Bernard M. Hoekman, The World Bank, Washington, USA and
Petros C. Mavriodis, Columbia University Law School, USA

Despite – or because of – its success, the WTO has recently become the focus of vociferous protests by anti-globalization activists. This book separates the facts from the propaganda and provides an accessible overview of the WTO's history, structure and policies as well as a discussion of the future of the organization. It also confronts the criticisms of the WTO and assesses their validity.

Contents
Introduction 1. A brief history of the world trading system 2. The WTO in a nutshell 3. The GATT 4. Services and intellectual property 5. Dispute settlement, transparency and plurilateral agreements 6. Developing countries and the WTO 7. Whither the trading system after Doha

June 2007: 216x138mm: 160pp
Hb: 978-0-415-41458-6: **£70.00**
Pb: 978-0-415-41459-3: **£19.99**

NEW TITLE
Commonwealth
Inter- and non-state contributions to global governance

Timothy M. Shaw, Royal Roads University and University of the West Indies

The inter-state and non-state Commonwealth networks are rather unknown features of contemporary "global governance" yet they play a key part in supporting it. This is a fascinating exploration of these crucial webs of influence and power.

Contents
Introduction 1. Commonwealth(s) – inter- and non-state 2. From decolonization to democratization 3. Commonwealths today 4. Commonwealths' discourses and directions 5. Commonwealths and the competition 6. Commonwealths and the future

October 2007: 216x138mm: 176pp
Hb: 978-0-415-35120-1: **£65.00**
Pb: 978-0-415-35121-8: **£14.99**

Routledge
Taylor & Francis Group

To order any of these titles
Call: +44 (0) 1264 34 3071
Fax: +44 (0) 1264 34 3005
Email: book.orders@routledge.co.uk

For further information visit:
www.routledge.com/politics

GLOBAL INSTITUTIONS SERIES

NEW TITLE

The African Union

Challenges of globalization, security, and governance

Samuel M. Makinda, Murdoch University
F. Wafula Okumu, Institute for Security Studies

A comprehensive examination of the work of the African Union (AU), with special emphasis on its capacity to meet the challenges of building and sustaining governance institutions and security mechanisms.

Contents
Introduction 1. The Organization of African Unity and mutual preservation 2. The African Union: meeting the challenge of globalization 3. Governance, democracy, and the rule of law 4. Security and peace building 5. Knowledge and development 6. Challenges of globalization, security, and governance

October 2007: 216x138mm: 232pp
Hb: 978-0-415-40350-4: **£65.00**
Pb: 978-0-415-40349-8: **£14.99**

NEW TITLE

The European Union

Clive Archer, Manchester Metropolitan University

While there are many textbooks about the European Union (EU), Clive Archer covers the essential elements of the EU clearly and concisely, outlining the key debates and issues it faces today.

Contents
Introduction 1. The debate on the nature of the EU 2. A brief history of European integration 3. Institutions and processes 4. The EU's domestic policies 5. The EU's external activities 6. Where to now?

January 2008: 216x138mm: 200pp
Hb: 978-0-415-37012-7: **£65.00**
Pb: 978-0-415-37011-0: **£14.99**

Routledge
Taylor & Francis Group

To order any of these titles
Call: +44 (0) 1264 34 3071
Fax: +44 (0) 1264 34 3005
Email: book.orders@routledge.co.uk

For further information visit:
www.routledge.com/politics